MOVING ON AFTER THE MOVES OUT

MOVES OUT

JIM CONWAY, Ph.D.
SALLY CONWAY, M.S.

INTERVARSITY PRESS
DOWNERS GROVE, ILLINOIS 60515

129235

InterVarsity Press® is the book-publishing division of InterVarsity Christian Fellowship®, a student movement active on campus at hundreds of universities, colleges and schools of nursing in the United States of America, and a member movement of the International Fellowship of Evangelical Students. For information about local and regional activities, write Public Relations Dept., InterVarsity Christian Fellowship, 6400 Schroeder Rd., P.O. Box 7895, Madison, WI 53707-7895.

All Scripture quotations, unless otherwise indicated, are taken from The Living Bible © 1971. Used by permission of Tyndale House Publishers, Inc., Wheaton, IL 60189. All rights reserved.

Cover photograph: Jim Whitmer

ISBN 0-8308-1643-7

Printed in the United States of America

Library of Congress Cataloging-in-Publication Data

Conway, Jim.
    Moving on after he moves out/Jim Conway, Sally Conway.
     p. cm.
    Includes bibliographical references (p.).
    ISBN 0-8308-1643-7
     1. Divorced women—United States—Life skills guides. 2. Divorced
women—United States—Psychology. 3. Divorce—United States—
Religious aspects—Christianity.   I. Conway, Sally.
    HQ834.C73 1995
    305.9'0653—dc20

                                              94-23856
                                                CIP

18	17	16	15	14	13	12	11	10	9	8	7	6	5	4	3	2	1
09	08	07	06	05	04	03	02	01	00	99	98	97	96	95			

Dedicated to
Vernon C. Grounds
President Emeritus, Denver Seminary
who first cared for us
and then
taught us to care for others

— Part One —

The Disintegration

Almost every day you hear of another marriage breaking up—people with whom you work, church friends, popular entertainers and national leaders. It's so common you almost become immune to the shock and pain—until it's *you!*

The reasons vary:

"I need something more exciting."

"Our love has died."

"I just don't want to be married anymore."

"It's too much responsibility—I can't handle it."

"My spouse isn't pulling his weight."

"She isn't the same person I married."

"I've met someone who makes me feel like I've never felt before."

Yes, it's painfully common these days. But when abandonment hits *you,* it's a unique experience that you go through in your own way. There is no formula to follow, and nobody can tell you exactly how to survive.

However, we do want to share with you some principles and hope. We will use Ann's story as a starting point. But adapt that example to your own circumstances.

This book is also for the person whose spouse still lives at home but who has emotionally abandoned the marriage and is not willing to work toward change. In these very painful circumstances, you can adapt some of the principles we discuss.

First, we will look at the "people cost" of abandonment—what it did to Ann and her children.

— 1 —

All Dressed Up–
But Nowhere
to Go

*E*VERYTHING WAS ARRANGED. FOR DAYS ANN HAD BEEN PLANNING for this special anniversary night out. She had arranged for the kids to be cared for. She had spent time at the beauty shop, getting her hair fixed and her nails done.

Now she pressed a few wrinkles out of the elegant new dress she had bought for the occasion. As she stepped into the warm shower, she thought about the great evening Bob and she would have together. Maybe this special night would revitalize their sagging sex life. She dabbed on body oil so that when Bob touched her hand or her knee he wouldn't feel the skin of a "thirtysomething" mother but that of a sensual woman who wanted him.

As she stepped out of the shower, she splashed on Bob's favorite cologne. Then she started the meticulous process of makeup and dressing.

Wow, it's a quarter to seven. Only a few minutes left until Bob gets home. He was working late and had told her he would change at the office. She tried not to be overcome with excitement or skyrocketing emotions—but she really felt like a teenage girl and wanted to giggle. This was going to be a terrific night!

As she finished putting on her lipstick, she asked herself, *Why don't we do this more often? I used to feel this enthusiasm and sparkle; why has it gone away? How did we get so overwhelmed with the mundane chores of survival—paying bills, taking care of the kids, going to church and attending business dinners? How did our marriage settle down to be so terribly, terribly ordinary and very, very boring?* Maybe they needed more celebration times like this so that she could experience this excitement more often.

It was nearly seven o'clock, the magic moment! She dabbed a few last touches of perfume in the special places that always drove Bob wild. She flipped out the light and walked toward the kitchen. As she passed the living room, she stopped in front of a large wall mirror. *Now there's a smashingly elegant lady,* she thought.

Ann felt confident—she knew she looked sensational. She was not a sixteen-year-old, wondering if the evening was going to be okay. She was a confident woman married to a great husband and raising two wonderful kids. She looked great, and she felt very sexy. She thought to herself, *I look so great, I'm going to blow Bob away. This is a night he will never, never forget.*

What's Wrong?

She went into the kitchen and tidied up a few things. As the minutes dragged on, she decided to make a couple of quick phone calls to people who had called earlier and left messages on the machine.

What's wrong? she thought. *It's 7:30. I wonder if something has happened—I wonder if Bob's okay. Now, now,* she said to herself, *don't panic. Bob is always teasing you about that. Don't start calling his office or the hospitals or the police station. Just give it some time. You know he said he had to work late. He probably just got stuck on the phone, or he couldn't get rid of a client. It's okay, just cool it; after all, he's worth the wait.*

Her emotions were hard to control when she sat doing nothing. She decided to get a head start on the kids' lunches for the next day. She could always quit as soon as Bob walked in the door.

Still her mind was racing with fearful questions of whether he was all right. It was now ten minutes until eight. *What's happened? What's going on?*

Eight o'clock. Now, no matter what Bob might say, she was going to start calling. She touched the automatic dial button for Bob's office. Six, seven, eight—eleven rings and no answer. *Something is definitely wrong.*

She got out the phone book and found the number for Memorial Hospital. It was the largest one and had a trauma unit. If he had been injured in an accident, that's where he'd likely be taken.

Come on, come on, answer the phone! Finally, an answer, but then came the endless switching from department to department. They checked everywhere; Bob had not been admitted to the hospital.

What is happening to our wonderful evening together? Has Bob gone off the road somewhere? Is he dying at this very moment? Am I going to be a widow?

Just then the front door opened, and Bob stepped in very quietly.

Ann was in panic. "Bob, I'm glad you're home! I've been so afraid something terrible had happened to you! What *did* happen? Why are you so late? I thought we were going out for our anniversary." A torrent of questions raced out of Ann's mouth.

Finally Bob said, "I think you need to sit down." Now Ann was really worried. *What's going on?* she wondered. They stepped into the living room, and Ann quickly sat down on the edge of a chair facing Bob.

Bob was quiet for a few moments that seemed like an eternity. Then he said, "Ann, this is not easy to say, but I'm leaving you. I want a divorce and I want it quickly. You and I have had nothing between us for years, and I need more. I'm in love with a woman from work—Jennifer. We've been seeing each other for about a year, and I intend to marry her."

Ann couldn't believe what she was hearing. She could feel her heart pounding in her chest. *This can't be true.* She felt dizzy. Her brain seemed locked onto the new dress she had bought, the special perfume that Bob liked and her warm, passionate feelings toward him. She couldn't speak a word. She was *all dressed up—with nowhere to go.*

Bob slowly started to get up. As if the last few minutes hadn't been crushing enough, he said quietly and firmly, "I'm going to pack a few things and then I'm leaving." He abruptly turned toward the bedroom.

Worse Than Death

As Ann stared at the indentation on the chair cushion where Bob had been sitting, she thought, *Moments ago we were husband and wife. Moments ago I was going to have the greatest night of my life.* But now, it was as if she had been thrown out of heaven and condemned forever to hell.

Her mind rejected what was happening. Certainly this was some horrible nightmare. She would soon wake up in a cold sweat of panic, only to find it was a terrible dream and Bob was sleeping quietly beside her.

Little did Ann realize that the rejection and humiliation she felt at this moment were just the tip of all she was to experience in the next days and months.

She heard movement behind her. Bob was coming quietly out of the bedroom with a small suitcase in his hand. Some jackets were thrown over his arm and he carried an extra pair of shoes in his left hand. He made his way to the front door, opened it and then turned to face Ann. "I'm sorry, but I guess I never really loved you."

I keep thinking of the good old days of the past, long since ended. Then my nights were filled with joyous songs. I search my soul and meditate upon the difference now. . . . I think of God and moan, overwhelmed with longing for his help. I cannot sleep until you act. I am too distressed even to pray! (Ps 77:5-6, 3-4)

— 2 —

The River
of
Destruction

*A*NN STOOD IN FRONT OF THE LIVING-ROOM CHAIR FOR A LONG TIME, stunned with shock and disbelief. She had watched the door close behind Bob and dimly remembered hearing his car start up and drive away. But she was feeling lightheaded and on the edge of fainting. She felt as unreal as when she was coming out from anesthesia following her major surgery last year.

Ann was usually a very confident and take-charge person, but the numbing shock left her absolutely powerless. She kept replaying the two contrasting scenes in her mind. The first was the deliriously happy scene of getting ready for their anniversary night. She had pictured it culminating in a long, passionate sexual episode before they drifted off to sleep.

The other scene was straight from the pit of hell, dreamed up by Satan himself. Who could have imagined that just as everything seemed so successful—two children, a nice house, good jobs—all of it would come tumbling down with a few phrases from Bob's mouth. "I want a divorce—I guess I never really loved you."

The "Other Woman"

As these two electrifying yet contradictory episodes kept racing through Ann's mind, they were punctuated by the humiliating realization that Bob was leaving her for another woman. She could hear the stinging words: "I'm in love with a woman from work—Jennifer. We've been seeing each other for about a year, and I intend to marry her."

Jennifer had come to Bob's company two years ago to head up the advertising division. Swiftly the images flashed back. Ann could remember Bob's comments about what a great job Jennifer was doing and "what a sparkle she is around the office." She also remembered how uneasy both Jennifer and Bob were when Bob introduced Jennifer to Ann at a company get-together.

Ann had never thought it would happen to her. But here she was, losing her husband to the dreaded "other woman." The scenes played over and over in her mind, with all their ugly words, every moment she was awake.

The next days were pure hell. Bob made no contact. She felt embarrassed and hesitant to tell friends or family, even her children. Kimberly, age twelve, and Shawn, age nine, didn't sense that anything was wrong. They thought their dad was just away on another long business trip. They did wonder a little why Mom seemed so sad, but they were preoccupied with school and friends, so they didn't worry much about her. But for Ann it seemed she was helplessly standing by while someone else was destroying everything that had given meaning to her life.

The Flood Of Losses

Each morning she woke to a stronger awareness of the massive losses she was experiencing. She realized she had lost not only her husband but also the position of being married. That identity was gone. It was as if she had put all of her money in a savings and loan and then, because of mismanagement, her investment was lost. Her entire emotional investment in Bob and her marriage had now been swept away.

She remembered the Midwest floods of 1993. Her friend Beth, who lived in one of the devastated areas, had graphically described what it was like standing on the dike. On the one side was the Mississippi River. On the other side were the little town that she loved and her home with all of her family's possessions.

Suddenly, about a hundred yards from where Beth stood, the dike failed, and the waters of the Mississippi clawed incessantly, churning the hole ever larger and larger. Beth could see her house as the "river monster," like a giant animal, swallowed things in the yard: the dog house, the play house, the lawn furniture. Then the detached garage started to move.

The car was swept away. The bushes and trees in their yard were gone. Now it was just their precious house and all of their belongings standing there as the river continued to devour.

Then the house—along with years of memory—began to shudder. It seemed as if the house was trying to run away from the water. It started to move, but then it collapsed. The roof was pushed ahead in the torrent. In the place of their dreams swirled twenty-five feet of water—and the roar of the "monster."

At the time, Ann had cried with Beth over her terrible loss. Now it was Beth's turn to weep with Ann. She was glad for her close friendship with Beth. As soon as Ann phoned and said, "I've got to talk to somebody I can trust," Beth said, "I'll call you back as soon as the kids are in bed."

Beth was an island in a sea of storm. Ann could pour it all out: "I'm devastated; Bob has abandoned me. I feel as if everything I've invested in all of these years has been swept away. I'm angry;

I wish I hadn't made the investment in Bob. I wish I could get even. It's humiliating! What will people think of me?"

But at the same time she wondered aloud to Beth, "What if it's my fault after all? Maybe I'm really to blame."

Who Will Remember?

As the days went by, Ann felt that her life was being washed away by a giant river flood. Not only had she missed an anniversary dinner—she was losing her history with Bob.

Were all the events of the past thirteen years suddenly to be washed away? Who could she share those things with, if not Bob? Who would understand all of the subtleties of the crazy fun things they had done together, the little traditions and secret jokes? The question that she kept asking in her mind was, *Who will remember?*

Yes, it was possible to tell someone how she had felt when she was first pregnant—the awful morning sickness, Bob's special way of rubbing her back to relieve the spasms, then the wonder of Kimberly's birth as Bob held Ann's hand. He had been her emotional encourager during that difficult time. Ann could recount all this to someone else, but only Bob would know the depths and details. *Yes,* she thought, *I can tell Kimberly what it was like when she was born. But it isn't the same as remembering with Bob.*

Suddenly ten thousand memories rushed through her mind, and she felt panicked. No other human being had been with her during these events. Bob was the only person with whom she could completely share, because he was the only other person who had been with her in those moments. Now he was gone.

Where Is Ann?

Bob's abandonment seemed larger and more awful with every passing day as Ann experienced each new loss. Her life kept tumbling out of control. She had lost her husband, her marriage, her emotional investment and her history. Now Ann was shocked to realize she was also losing her emotional stability.

She was a strong woman. She had worked through other hard things. But now three weeks had gone by since Bob had left. She was continuing to pour out her heart to a few close friends and sharing her pain with us in counseling, but she was feeling worse instead of better.

She was having trouble at work. People were starting to ask, "Ann, are you okay?" She was just putting in her time and feeling guilty because she was not really being productive.

The same was true at home. She was simply throwing meals together; the house was a mess; the laundry was piling up except for a few things that she washed each week. She wasn't opening the mail or paying any bills. The kids now were asking where Dad was. At first she evaded their questions, but they would not be put off.

When they learned their dad was really *gone,* they too felt abandoned, hurt and angry. They began to have trouble with schoolwork, were explosive with each other and even hinted at running away. Finally Ann told them the basic facts about where their dad was and tried to help them work through the turmoil. But she knew this was one kind of pain she could not remove for them. This went far beyond Band-Aids.

What was wrong? It felt as if her car's steering wheel suddenly had come off in her hands and her brakes had failed. She couldn't stop the car and she couldn't steer it. Her life was out of control. But she didn't crash just once; she had disaster after disaster.

Who Pays the Bills?

Ann was facing deep financial problems. It had taken both of their salaries to cover the payments on the house, the two cars, tuition for the kids in private school and all of the other bills. Yet she had had no contact with Bob, and he had not yet sent any money. *How am I supposed to pay the bills?* she wondered.

Bob had said in passing, that terrible night when he walked out, "I'm moving into an apartment." Now she realized that their income, which barely made ends meet, was going to have to cover an extra apartment, phone and utilities. Plus he was probably spending money on Jennifer. Ann recalled with indignation how Bob used money to impress people. She was sure he was doing the same with Jennifer.

So that's why he's not sending any money or making any contact, she fumed. *He's spending his salary on Jennifer and his apartment.* "No!" she yelled out loud, "he's not spending *his* money—he's spending *our* money on Jennifer!"

Ann felt like a live volcano. She would explode if Bob walked through the door this moment. She wasn't sure what she would do, but one thing was clear—she would read Bob the riot act! She would verbally tear him limb from limb. He had not only abandoned her; he had also stuck her with all the bills!

On the advice of several people, Ann took the painful step of contacting a lawyer. They began the process of deciding how to pressure Bob for financial help. She had finally opened all the bills and paid as many as she could. But as of the first of the month, it would be either the mortgage or the groceries and car payment (or taking money out of savings, and she was scared to start doing that).

She was living in no man's land. She was not really married, nor was she divorced.

In-laws or Outlaws?

She called Bob at work, but he became very angry and wouldn't talk to her. She decided to try to find out where he was living, hoping that if she contacted him away from his work he might be more cooperative. So she called Bob's mom, who had been a close friend to Ann.

"Hi, Mom, this is Ann," she said in her most cheery voice. "I really need your help." She tried to control her emotions, but suddenly it all started to spill out. "You probably know by now that Bob has moved out—I don't know where he is, he hasn't contacted me and I need to talk to him regarding finances. Can you give me his phone number?"

Ann could sense Mom's hesitation. She was startled to feel a distance and coolness. *Maybe it really is true that blood runs thicker than water, especially in a crisis.*

Reluctantly Bob's mom said, "I'm not sure I'm supposed to tell you where Bob is living."

Ann pleaded, "But Mom, you and I have been such good friends—you've got to help me. I can't call him at work because you know how angry he gets. I'm not asking you to take sides, but there's no way I can make the mortgage payment and take care of the kids if I don't get some help from Bob. Please help me."

There was a long pause, and then the hesitant answer, "He's living at Willow Lakes apartments." She gave her Bob's phone number and then concluded by saying, "Ann, I'm sorry for both of you, but it's probably best that you and I not talk again."

Will the river ever stop sweeping me away? Ann cried to herself. She not only had lost her husband, her married status, her emotional investment in their history together, her ability to function as a confident woman in control and her financial stability, but also she had lost a close friend, Bob's mother. The river of abandonment was smashing every part of her life.

It took Ann two days to get up her courage to call Bob at his apartment. She was afraid Jennifer would answer. After thinking through dozens of scenarios about what to say, depending on who would answer, she finally called.

Fortunately, Bob did answer the phone. He was cool, distant, businesslike and abrupt. He did not ask how she was doing or how the children were. He didn't even ask how she was explaining to the kids that he had been gone more than a month. He just grudgingly said, "I'll cover the payment on the house and on my car. You have to cover the utilities and everything else."

Ann started to protest. But Bob broke in, "You're lucky you're getting that much. I could have just left town."

Who Can Be Trusted?

When will this nightmare end? Ann asked herself. *Will these terrible losses keep coming?* She sat trembling as all of her losses were replaying in her mind. She needed to talk to someone. Maybe it was time to swallow her pride and call her parents.

As their phone rang, she wished she had a closer relationship with them. They had always seemed to like Bob, and they had been supportive of her marriage, but she had never been able to share meaningfully with them. Conversations were usually limited to her folks' health, her kids' progress in school and the recent hot or cold spell.

As her mother answered the phone, the accumulated weeks of stress, abandonment, rejection and loss after loss totally overwhelmed Ann. She sobbed and sobbed. Her mother tried to comfort her, aware that something terrible had happened but not knowing what.

Finally, Ann was able to blurt out, "Bob has left me. He moved out more than a month ago. He's going to marry a woman from work named Jennifer. He's just abandoned me and the kids. I don't know what I'm going to do."

Suddenly, her mother's voice became angry. "I never did like Bob, but I was afraid to tell you. I always had a suspicion that he was seeing other women. He took too many long trips that seemed unnecessary. He seems like a sneaky person who would lie and never give it a second thought."

At first Ann welcomed the words—*at least Mom is on my side.* But then she began to feel uneasy. As her mother attacked Bob, she was also indirectly attacking Ann's choices and their thirteen years of marriage.

When her dad picked up the phone, he continued the barrage against Bob. After Ann hung up, she realized she was experiencing yet another loss. Her parents were losing the objectivity she had thought she could depend on. They couldn't be counted on to help heal her marriage. Their bitterness at Bob would not help Ann recover.

Fifth Wheel

Ann cried herself to sleep that night after talking to her parents. But by the next morning she was determined to take charge of her shattered life and try to pull some things together. It was Thursday, the night when she and Bob usually ate with several other couples at a local restaurant.

As she left for work that Thursday morning, she decided she would meet with her old friends that evening. The decision gave her a new lease on life. She was able to be more productive at work and more in control of her emotions. Maybe things were finally going to get a little better.

That evening she walked into the restaurant and began a round of hugging and greeting her friends. They seemed glad to see her and said they had missed her. But about halfway through the hugging process, one of the women put it directly to her, "Where's Bob? Is he working again or out of town?"

She wasn't going to protect him any longer. These people were her friends and they would help her through this time. Ann responded quietly, "Bob and I are separated. He moved out about a month ago and plans to marry Jennifer, a young woman he works with."

Suddenly their corner of the restaurant was silent. People

stopped hugging and greeting. A strange mixture of conflicting glances, whispered comments and gestures took place. Immediately, some of the people tried to console Ann. Others attacked Bob. The rest simply took their places around the table, looked at the menus and started to order their food.

Somehow Ann got through the meal. It was certainly not what she expected. She had hoped for the good times of laughing and sharing together. Instead, it was a painful reminder of another loss she was experiencing.

The river of destruction was continuing to erode her life. Even though some of the people still liked her, she did not feel really welcome in this couples' group. She was no longer part of a couple. But she wasn't single either. Bob's abandonment had instantly transported her to a strange country where no one knew her nor she them. It was as if she couldn't speak the language and seemed unable to connect with anyone.

Careless Christians

Ann staggered through the rest of the week. By Saturday evening she had decided she was going to be tough and go to church for the first time. Oh, she had been there many times before without Bob, when he was on one of those famous "business trips." (Was her mother right? Were those trips planned just so Bob could spend extra time with Jennifer? Had there been other women before Jennifer?)

Her mind raced with all kinds of wild imaginations. But none of those questions was going to stop her; she was going to go to church tomorrow. Certainly her Christian friends would be able to handle what was happening and give her some support.

Ann casually greeted a few people as she entered the church. She enjoyed the music. The message was irrelevant to what she was struggling with, but she hoped it was helpful to someone. Her real problems came after the service at the extended fellowship time.

She received the same reaction here as from her friends at the restaurant. Some reached out to console her while others drew back or used a pet phrase to help them quickly exit the scene, "We'll be praying for you."

Will they really pray? Ann wondered sarcastically. *Or are they just using Christian lingo to avoid really caring about me?*

As the weeks went by, she began to notice a pattern taking place with the church people. Some wanted to console her, but others treated her with a hint of suspicion, as if they thought she must have done something to make Bob leave.

She also noticed that her couple friends—both church people and nonchurch—didn't know how to relate to her since she was no longer part of a couple. In fact, she felt absolutely certain some of the men were trying to hit on her. One guy even went so far as to suggest that he'd be glad to help if she needed a man to put his arms around her or "whatever." She felt shock and revulsion.

Ann intuitively sensed that married women were threatened by her. Some of the wives began to treat her as if she were out to get their husbands. When Ann and Bob had been at events together, these women had felt their husbands were safe. Now that Ann was a separated woman, they put her into the category of a woman on the prowl who would do anything to get a man. Ann felt very awkward—not truly married or truly single.

After four or five weeks of trying to relate to all of her old, familiar groups, she was forced to realize that Bob's abandonment had caused another loss in her life. She had lost the Thursday night dinner group and her couple friends at the church. The river had taken more from her. Would this be the last?

It's Take-Charge Time
With time, Ann gained more strength. By sheer grit she decided

to press forward with two simultaneous plans of attack. First, she was going to hope for, pray for and work toward her marriage being reestablished. Second, she planned to take better control of her life. She had slipped into a habit of eating irregularly, and often it was junk food. She started eating healthy meals and taking a daily walk.

She also arranged her schedule so she could spend priority time with several of her women friends who seemed to genuinely understand what she was going through. These women were willing to help her survive this abandonment and, at the same time, not push her to give up on Bob and their marriage.

She also continued regular counseling with us to find out why this had happened, what they each had contributed and what she could do to be a better marriage partner—if and when Bob would ever want to reconsider their relationship.

Who Understands?
But as Ann worked hard on her new losses, she experienced another loss that she never expected. It was the loss of understanding by her children. A new explosive anger and hostility flashed between Shawn and Kim and toward Ann and Bob. Ann discovered that both of her children were also deeply angry at God, whom they blamed for allowing the separation to happen.

Ann also noticed a change in the children's attitude toward Bob and Ann's marriage. It came in the form of innocent questions: "Why did Dad leave? Didn't he like you anymore, Mom? Did you do something that made Dad angry?"

Ann realized that her own children were carrying the same questions and suspicions toward her as did many of the church people. Kim and Shawn resented not only their dad for leaving, but also their mom, because they thought in some way she had also caused the marriage failure. Here was another loss. The destructive river of Bob's abandonment was still churning—her close, trusting relationship with her children was unstable now.

Ann truly was in no man's land—not divorced, not a never-married, not legally separated—but not married either. Her plight could be compared to that of stroke victims. Their bodies don't work. They want to get out of bed and walk, but one whole side of the body is paralyzed. Stroke victims often wish they could die. They long for the final stroke to end life. For now they are between two worlds. No longer can they live a full life, but neither have they been released through death.

Stuck between two worlds, facing loss after loss after loss, Ann asked, *Will the river of Bob's abandonment ever stop sweeping away my life?*

Come, Lord, and show me your mercy, for I am helpless, overwhelmed, in deep distress; my problems go from bad to worse. Oh, save me from them all! See my sorrows; feel my pain; forgive my sins. (Ps 25:16-18)

— 3 —

The Roses
Are Dead—
But the Thorns
Still Cut

*B*Y NOW IT WAS LATE FALL. ANN GOT THE CLIPPERS FROM THE GARAGE and began to trim back the roses in preparation for their grand display in the spring.

It felt good to be working, to be making progress, to be cleaning up something. But as she moved around the rose bushes, carefully pruning, her arms were repeatedly scratched when thorns jabbed through her shirt. As she stepped back another thorn got her elbow. Then her pants got caught in another bush and thorns found their mark on her leg.

Ann took a break and sat down on the retaining wall. As she carefully pulled out a couple of thorns that had become embedded in her arm, she realized this was a picture of what she was going through in real life.

The rose blossoms had been killed by the frost, but the thorns were still there, able to do their damage. Each little puncture was in danger of becoming infected and leaving a sore red mark for days to come.

Ann looked around her yard. She felt so different about this house lately. It used to be a place of joy and promise, but now it was a place of nightmares. Everything was a constant reminder that the roses in her life had died.

You Owe Me!

Sitting there, she began to identify some of the feelings she had been wrestling with these past few months. (We had encouraged Ann to remember her feelings and make a written list.)

It was easy to identify *shock,* her reaction when Bob told her he wanted out of the marriage. It was also easy to distinguish her feeling of *numbness* as Bob casually said he was going to marry Jennifer. *Panic* was another feeling that Ann recognized. It had come in those early minutes of Bob's announcement, and it was not a feeling that was going away easily.

She thought about how *angry* she was at Bob. It wasn't just anger—it was rage. At times she wanted to tear him apart. She felt a strong desire to punish Bob—to get even with him. The phrase kept going around in her mind, *You owe me! You made a promise! You can't just abandon me and the children this way!*

The Special Porsche

Ann thought about the woman in Florida who had put an ad in the paper to start the process of selling an almost new car. The ad read, "Fully loaded, almost new Porsche, $3,500." A prospective buyer saw the ad night after night, but thought it was a misprint or it must be a wrecked car, so he never bothered to call the woman.

After two weeks of seeing the ad in the paper, he decided to make a call. The woman assured him that the car was in showroom condition and fully loaded. The man asked, "And the price is $3,500?" The woman responded, "That's right." In a matter of minutes the man was at the house. The immaculate car was sitting on the front lawn. It was spotless. It was beautiful. The man went to the front door and asked, "Is this the Porsche that you're selling for $3,500?" The woman responded, "Yes, it is. Would you like to take a drive?"

The man eagerly jumped at the opportunity and took the car on a test run. It was like brand new. It even had that "new car" smell. It was just what he was looking for. But could it be true that this car, worth over $35,000, could be selling for $3,500?

Again he asked the woman, "You're selling this car for $3,500?" She said yes. He wrote out a check; she signed the pink slip and handed it to him. The man quickly drove off. He was afraid she would change her mind.

Two weeks later he called the woman again, identifying himself as the man who had bought her car. She responded, "Oh, no, is something wrong with it?"

"No, not at all, everything is fine, it's wonderful. But I must ask, why you were willing to sell that car for $3,500? You must know that it's worth over $35,000."

She said, "My husband ran off to the Bahamas with his secretary and told me as he left, 'Sell my car and send me the money.' "

Ann smiled and thought, *There must be some creative way for me to get even with Bob for what he has done. Maybe there's some way to leave him penniless so he won't be able to flit around the country with Jennifer as he is doing now.*

Which Is the Real Ann?

In the midst of her thoughts of revenge, Ann recognized some of the other dark feelings that she'd experienced since that terrible anniversary night. She wondered if she would ever recover from this prolonged *depression*—this sense of hopelessness and despair. She was glad that God was keeping his arms around her, because many, many times she battled thoughts of suicide. *After all*, she thought to herself, *if heaven is such a wonderful place, why shouldn't I be there and escape this hell that I'm living in now?*

But each time she toyed with the idea of suicide, she was smacked in the face with guilt. How could she so easily cop out, letting her children face the abandonment all on their own? She felt deeply ashamed for even thinking such thoughts.

It was as if there were many different Anns. One Ann wanted to restore the marriage and to help Bob, who seemed so confused. Another Ann was deeply depressed, shamed, full of guilt, almost immobilized. And still another Ann was raging with anger, wanting to punish Bob, vowing to make him pay for abandoning her and the children. Would this fragmented Ann ever come together? Would there ever be a oneness in her feelings?

Abandonment Déjà Vu

After one particularly demanding day at work, she recognized that her self-confidence had really slipped. She didn't seem to be able to take charge of things as she used to. In fact, she wondered if her coping skills were going away. She was also having trouble connecting with people. She kept asking herself, *Is it me or is it them?*

Sad memories began to flood in. Junior high is tough for any girl, but Ann remembered how the kids had picked on her because she was skinny. Worse than that, it was when she was in junior high that her father had divorced her mother. The feelings of her father's abandonment were now being replayed.

She remembered all of the times of dating, thinking a certain guy was the greatest—and then being dropped. *Why did it always seem that I loved the boys more than they loved me?* she asked herself. *Why was I always desperately reaching out for love?* Even when she gave in sexually, she had never felt any security. The teenage boyfriends, and later the adult boyfriends, had all left her.

But it had seemed so different with Bob. When they met in college, it appeared as if there was an equality of love and commitment to each other. *Finally,* Ann thought to herself, *I've found a man who is not going to abandon me.*

As Ann remembered all the hope she had placed in Bob, she experienced a deep, deep sadness. Just like all the other men—Bob abandoned her.

Abandonment's Awful Harvest

Thousands of women are abandoned in one way or another each day. The abandoned woman has lots of sad company. And they all have in common, to some extent, certain changes in the ways they feel, think and function.

In a journal article about abandonment, Faith H. Leibman lists some of the common feelings and reactions of people who are abandoned:

☐ Continually threatened by others' comments and actions
☐ Suspicion and mistrust
☐ Withdrawal from the outside world
☐ Self-centeredness
☐ Feelings of entitlement
☐ Fear of failure
☐ Inability to share feelings or to develop a respect for others' feelings and needs
☐ Preoccupation with own needs and desires
☐ Anger at others for apparent rejection[1]

These patterns tend to result in a great deal of frustration and anger. People going through such a deep loss find their relationships changing in ways they don't like yet are unable to control.

If this is your experience, don't be depressed by this temporary change in you. Eventually you will be able to move on and be a healthy person.

Frequently, the abandoned woman has no one to talk to. In Ann's situation, even though she was feeling all of the terrible feelings, it was difficult for her to call even her close friends and tell them the full story of what was happening. After all, everyone thought that Bob and Ann were the ideal couple, and they each held positions in their local church. So at first she kept up the front that their marriage was okay.

Besides, Ann wasn't sure what was going to happen. Maybe this would be a temporary thing with Bob. At first she hoped he would only be gone overnight. Then, maybe he would only be gone a few days. She kept saying to herself, *maybe, maybe.* Her hope kept her from reaching out to get help from very many people. Like many who are abandoned, she bore the pain and anguish of those first days basically alone.

Secret Tears in Churchyards

Women need to ask for help—right from the start. But, sadly, for some women it is days or weeks before they honestly connect with another human being and finally start to get support to survive this horrible experience. We encourage you to reach out immediately for the help you need from friends, a lawyer, a pastor, a counselor—and God.

One woman told us that when her husband left, she was totally at a loss and absolutely without anyone to comfort her—because no one else knew. She said, "I would get in my car and drive around for hours. Sometimes I'd pull into a church parking lot and just sit there weeping. I hoped someone would find me crying and ask the simple question, 'Why are you crying? Is there anything I can do to help?' "

Then she told us, "I've wondered, since then, how many

abandoned woman are driving around the cities of our country, weeping, wishing someone would reach out and ask, 'Can I help?' "

You have seen me tossing and turning through the night. You have collected all my tears and preserved them in your bottle! You have recorded every one in your book. The very day I call for help, the tide of battle turns. My enemies flee! This one thing I *know: God is for me!* (Ps 56:8-9)

— Part Two —

The Disposable Woman

Most people reading this much of Ann's story would become very angry over the pain she had to go through as Bob disposed of her and continued his affair with Jennifer.

As we begin this section, it's important to remember:

1. We've only told you Ann's part of the story. We've not heard anything from Bob—his perspective on his leaving; factors in his past that predisposed him to such a decision; his view of the reasons why Ann became "disposable" in his eyes.

2. The focus of this book is not so much on *what ought to be* or *what is right*, but rather *what is*.

One of the traps that women get into as they experience abandonment is to think only in terms of *what ought to be* instead of *what is*. Typically, a woman will strongly feel, and probably say, "You owe me; this isn't right; we planned our whole lives together and now you've changed the rules."

Of course it isn't right! So it is perfectly natural for a woman to feel this way; she has every right to be indignant, jealous—and full of rage. Yet even though those feelings are there, the woman needs to face the reality of *what is*. Reality is that she is being abandoned.

She must understand why she is being demolished so that she will know how to rebuild her life and her future. In chapter four we will look at the times, or seasons, in life when a woman might be abandoned. Chapter five will examine several other kinds of abandonment that can happen to a woman to set her up for abandonment before or after marriage. Chapter six will look at the changes in her and her husband that sometimes cause a husband to see his wife as "disposable" and to leave her.

—— 4 ——

When a
Woman Becomes
Disposable

STAGES OF COUPLE RELATIONSHIPS CAN BE COMPARED TO CHILD development. Children react to their parents and other people in predictable ways at certain ages. For example, we expect a young baby to cling to the mother. And we expect both the mother and the baby to enjoy their strong, loving connection.

We've all heard of the "terrible twos" as the child says "No!" to almost everything. The child has a need to be independent from the parents but never wanders too far from them.

The teen years commonly are marked by rebellion and doing everything opposite from the parents. Often teens say, "I don't care if I never see my parents again."

Finally, somewhere in the child's twenties, the parents become "intelligent" again as the child gets started into adulthood and sees life from a new perspective. The child is able to appreciate the parents and yet enjoy independence from them.

Couple relationships are often as predictable as a child's development.

First is the romantic, passionate time when the couple is inseparable and each is nourished by the other. In this stage, neither sees any flaws in the other: "Oh, I love you in glasses; you look so intelligent," or "Some of the greatest people in history have been short."

Then follows the separation yet closeness stage. Each person must make sure he or she is still a unique individual: "John, I just need more time to myself for reading—I miss that. Don't feel rejected; I just need this part of my life as well."

Outright rebellion similar to the teen years often comes next. We commonly get letters with statements such as, "He is exactly the opposite of all he used to stand for. He used to be a good husband, a leader in the church and a very thoughtful person. Now he doesn't go to church—he drinks and hangs out at a singles' bar and treats me like dirt." Or the rebellion may take a milder form, showing up as a desire to have separate activities and more privacy—a kind of secrecy with less information shared.

Finally the couple reestablishes a relationship of friendship, respect and love. They are not as enmeshed with each other as in the first romantic days, but they are companions. They have come to value both their couple similarities and their individual differences. Each allows the other freedom to be himself or herself, yet they each choose to be marriage partners. They are no longer leaning on each other or pulling away, but they are walking next to each other.

At any of these natural developmental stages a marriage can fall apart, as one or both feel that they have made a bad choice or that since the addictive romance is gone, their marriage is doomed. They can be helped if they see it's only a normal phase that ultimately will lead to health. Sadly, some people move from partner to partner, looking for the mythical magical mate.[1]

Just as abandonment may take place at several points in the marriage's emotional development, so also there are special ages in life when abandonment is more likely. "Seasons of abandonment" are somewhat predictable. It's similar to predicting the probability of a snowstorm sometime during January or February in the city of Chicago. It's also easy to predict that Chicago will not likely have a snowstorm during July or August.

It is crucial to understand that the seasonal changes of life, for either wife or husband, *do not cause* abandonment, but an abrupt or even normal life change can create an environment where abandonment could be more likely. The people involved are the ones who decide how they will react to each life change. A life change is not a matter for shame or despair but a time of choice.

The First Year of Marriage

The greatest likelihood of marital breakup is during the first year of marriage. Two people are trying to blend their lives to create something that never existed before—their unique marriage. Thousands of adjustments take place as couples think through how to earn money and who decides how to spend it. They also must establish how to relate to in-laws, how to build couple friendships and what to do with their former single friends. They have to think through where to live, what to own, leisure activities, sexual adjustments, when and if to have children, and how involved to be in their community and church.

Each one of these and thousands of other decisions require value judgments. Each partner is wrestling with thoughts such as, *If we make this decision, what does that mean to me? Do I want to place that much of my/our time or money in this area?*

In the first year the typical couple is totally blown away by the mountain of decisions and value discussions that need to take place in order to form this new entity—their marriage.

As conflicts begin to erupt, almost every spouse wonders if he or she made a bad choice of a marriage partner. People are drawn together by physical attraction, emotional chemistry and a growing appreciation of the other person. But the whole dating scenario is really a performance dance. We generally show only our good side—"I don't want him to see me without my makeup," or "She loves it when I show up with flowers."

During the first one or two years, the married couple needs to make the transition from lust to love and finally to commitment. If the commitment level has grown before the couple actually gets married and both of them are determined to stay together even through rough times, then, as they solve problem after problem, the adjustments become a verification that they can make their marriage work.

However, if the relationship has not developed a strong commitment during that first year of marriage, lust and attraction will not be strong enough to hold them together as they are bombarded by the thousands of first-year choices.

One or both of the partners may feel that they've made a mistake. They miss the romance, the mad sexual desire, the excitement and the challenge of the hunt. They miss pursuing and being pursued. They never expected that marriage would settle down and become so ordinary, with the need for lots of *work* on communication and conflict resolution.

So, consciously or unconsciously, they begin to look around. Tragically, some partners try to find elsewhere the same feelings they had before marriage—and when they think they have found it in someone new, abandonment can take place.

Abandonment appears first as an emotional pulling away from the partner. Then follow the more obvious indicators such as avoidance through work, excessive play, an affair or separation.

Sometimes the basic reason for first-year abandonment is that the couple was not prepared for marriage in the first place. They did not practice resolving problems before they were married; they assumed that the nagging doubts they each felt would simply melt away when they were married.

Seven-Year Itch

A second common time when abandonment may take place is when a couple nears the end of their twenties, about year seven or eight of their marriage. At this stage people wonder if they are accomplishing the goals they mentally set up in their late teens or early twenties. At each stage of life, similar questions are being raised. Who am I? Does my life have meaning? Who are the people I want to relate to? And how does God fit into my life? If they are not on target with their personal goals, the spouse may be blamed and the marriage threatened.

Mark and Julie, who married in their early twenties, are examples of this seven-year stress. They always talked in generalities about what they wanted out of life. Mark was a very ambitious young man who started climbing the corporate ladder. He liked the fast track. He enjoyed wearing hand-tailored suits; he was willing to go in over his head financially in order to drive a Mercedes; he wanted the image. He was sure that by the time he was in his thirties he would be a vice president.

Mark wasn't opposed to having a child, but he didn't fully understand that Julie's goals were to have three or four children. The first child didn't cause a great deal of trauma in their marriage, but after number three, Mark really began to feel the financial pressure and time squeeze. He wanted Julie to be available for him, and he felt increasingly uncomfortable when her time was taken up by the children's demands.

He expected Julie to help him climb the corporate ladder, not slow him down. He had always thought she would be available for business dinners and for travel. In short, she was to be his public relations person to help him be a vice president by age thirty-two and company president by forty-two.

During Mark's thirtieth year, Julie became pregnant again. Mark was deeply angry and blamed Julie. "This is what happened the last time you got pregnant. You said maybe you didn't have the diaphragm in right or not enough contraceptive jelly! What is it with you? When are you going to learn that I don't want any more children?"

For the next several weeks Mark badgered Julie about getting an abortion. He did not want a fourth child. In fact, he didn't want child number two or three. It wasn't that he didn't like the children—they were a strain on his plans and directions. Julie refused to consider an abortion and started to act as if she were superwoman. Even though her days were exhausting, she no longer asked Mark to do anything around the house or with the children. She renewed her offer to go with him to business dinners to help his career.

But her initiative didn't work. Mark responded by withdrawing. He spent more and more time at work, frequently accepting company assignments in distant cities. He intentionally started the process of withdrawing and abandoning. He reasoned, *If she doesn't care about my desires, why should I care about hers?*

Yes, they were still married, but Mark had emotionally deserted Julie because the reality of his marriage and family was not matching his personal life goals. Nor were his assumptions matching Julie's goals. At this stage, either they were going to settle into a life of pretense in order not to disturb Mark's career advancement or this emotional abandonment would be a prelude to separation and divorce.

Mid-Life Abandonment
A third point when abandonment may occur is at mid-life.

The fortieth birthday is an important marker for most people. It's a watershed year. People are looking back at where they've been and ahead to where they're going. They ask, *How well am I doing? What do I need to accomplish in these next few years? How should I readjust my life now that I'm beginning to see things differently from when I was in my twenties?*

Typically, mid-life men are becoming more person- and feeling-oriented. They're wanting to connect with old friends. They wish they had a better connection with their kids. And there's a desire to replay some of the good parts of their lives. Frequently they have a new concern about their physical bodies that pushes them into exercise and weight-loss programs.

The fortyish man is in a crash program of reassessment. In his twenties and early thirties he was future-oriented. He knew where he wanted to go and he was willing to put out the effort to achieve his goals. But those goals were always down the road, and he pacified himself by saying, *When I'm older, I will achieve those goals.*

Now he *is* older. He doesn't feel satisfied with his life, and he realizes he doesn't have enough time to accomplish what he really wants. He experiences a near panic state. Change has to happen now!

He also begins to ask the "What if?" questions. *What if I had taken a different path? What if I had married a different woman? What if I didn't have kids? What if I had accepted those promotions that were offered to me, requiring me to move to another part of the country?*

He starts to question all of his life. *Who am I? What is life all about? What kind of work should I be doing? Shall I just go to Tahiti like Gauguin and follow my dream of painting? Maybe I'll sail around the world in my own sailboat. I could sell the business and buy a great cruising sailboat.*

47

But then he becomes painfully aware of all of his obligations: his company, his wife, his children, his responsibilities at church and the community committees he serves on.

Who am I? What should I be doing with my life? With whom should I relate? Does God know what I'm struggling with? Or perhaps he asks, *Does God even exist?*

In this setting of turmoil, confusion and panic, the mid-life man experiences some final straw that breaks his back and causes him to run.

Endless Demands

John was a certified public accountant, working for a large firm. He was glad his clientele was growing, and he didn't seem to mind the long hours. But by the time he reached mid-life, the needs of his family had drastically risen. It had happened ever so gradually, but now he was paying a large mortgage for his five-bedroom home, plus another mortgage for a cottage at a nearby lake. In addition, he was putting his oldest son through college and paying for all of the kids' special lessons in music, gymnastics and art.

In order to keep up with the expanding financial demands, John started moonlighting in the evening and on weekends. He told himself it would be no big deal. He had worked hard when he was in school and had survived. But he was not a schoolboy now. In his middle forties, he couldn't stand the stress.

He began to resent his accounting job, his son in college, the big house, the special lessons for the family. In fact, he began to resent his family—and especially his wife. *Why can't she do something? Why do I have to carry the whole load? She is just along for the good life I provide.*

Dangerous Ground

Marie worked in the same office as John. She had just been

divorced. She was also hungry for companionship and so was willing to listen as John poured out his anxiety. It was perfectly clear, from her needy perspective, that John's family was exploiting him. Marie sided with John and—hearing only John's side of the story—imagined that they were taking advantage of this kind, wonderful man.

Marie came into his office one day and found him staring out the window. His cheeks were wet with tears. He seemed like a sad little child or a lost puppy. Then Marie stepped across a boundary. She went behind his desk, put her hand on his shoulder and said, "John, what's wrong? Can I help?"

Like a drowning man, he reached out for her, put his arms around her, pulled her onto his lap and hugged her. Over the next several weeks they crossed all emotional, spiritual, sexual and marital boundaries. They were in a full-fledged affair.

John's problem was that he found himself overwhelmed with life. He was not achieving his life goals. He had run out of energy; he had no one to talk to; unconsciously his values and needs were changing. He had never spent any time thinking about how he was changing or making the necessary adaptations. Nor was he even aware of these changes enough to tell his wife that he was becoming a different man.

John and Marie were extremely vulnerable to each other. Because she was younger than John, she also fulfilled his fantasy to be younger himself. They were like moths drawn to a candle flame.

Often the wives of mid-life men whose husbands are involved in affairs are shocked by the drastic changes in their husband. On the one hand, he seems to have become a crazed philanderer, chasing after any young skirt. On the other hand, he is a sobbing little boy, running home to mother for comfort after being pulverized by a bunch of bullies.

The abandonment at mid-life is related to the gradual demise of the marriage relationship, but it is also strongly related to the life cycle development and reassessment taking place in both the man and the woman.

Menopause

A fourth point when change may bring on abandonment is when the wife reaches menopause.

"It's a joke; it's not real; it's women's imagination. What's the big deal? Snap out of it. Get over it," are the responses of some men about menopause. "It's a woman's problem. She needs to deal with it like any problem a businessman might have at work. Make a decision, act on it and it's solved." Oh, really?

During the time I (Sally) was going through menopause, I was acting very strangely. I would cry over what seemed to be nothing. Small problems that I had handled effortlessly before seemed to be uncontrollable monsters. I easily got rattled, confused and frustrated.

Our three daughters were in their teens or early twenties and understood that I was going through menopause. They realized I had to struggle to keep my emotions on an even keel. In order to help lighten the situation and still express a sense of caring, they began to call me by a new nickname, "Meno Mama."

When things seemed to get out of hand and I was starting to come apart, they would put their arms around me and say, "Oh, Mom, it's okay—you're just acting like a Meno Mama." Often that was enough to give me the assurance I needed and to alert me that this frazzled mood I had was not my normal way of looking at life.

The emotional highs and lows—and sometimes the unreasonableness—of a woman at menopause are better understood than they used to be. However, many husbands are surprised by the sexual change that occurs in their wives. A gradual decrease in a woman's hormones takes place, a decrease that may affect not only her emotions but also her skin tissue and her sexual drive. A woman may have decreased vaginal lubrication, along with shrinking vaginal tissue and diminishing breasts. She may also experience less desire to have sex.

Putting all these pieces together, you could have a woman who is unusually irritable, whose emotional responses change by the minute, and for whom sex is painful and endured only because it's her responsibility. Just at this time when she needs more sensitive understanding than ever from her mate, he may be totally confused and turned off by "the way she is acting lately."[2]

We have noticed that many couples in a difficult menopausal passage tend to follow one of three directions.

1. An avoidance type of abandonment may occur. They still live together, are still apparently a couple to all outward appearances, but their intimacy level has dropped to a very low level. They tolerate each other and decide that a divorce or an affair would be too costly or emotionally traumatic. Therefore, they just put up with an empty relationship.

2. One or both partners get involved in an affair. Most affairs at this age are to prove virility. Both men and women are trying to demonstrate to themselves that they are sexually attractive. They are answering the question *Can I still do it?* Sometimes the affair also becomes a way to manipulate the partner into more marital intimacy and commitment.

3. Both the husband and wife recognize they have a problem—that is, menopause—and they commit themselves to understand all they can about this passage in life and about each other. This, of course, is the healthiest and happiest direction to take. Their sexual life may be very different from when they were twenty-five years old. But less sexual frequency is not a deterrent when combined with a greater tenderness of cuddling and a deeper understanding of each other's needs.

Pre-retirement Abandonment

A fifth point when abandonment may occur, sadly, is around retirement.

Don and Millie had talked often about how great retirement was going to be. They were going to do all the things they had always wanted. It was going to be wonderful not having to work.

Unfortunately, neither of them was very specific about what they wanted to do in retirement. When Don and Millie were first married, they had many things in common, but in one area they were very dissimilar. Don was an outdoor, athletic person, and Millie didn't like outdoor sports at all.

Throughout their marriage they had mild disagreements about vacations. To Don, a vacation was white-water rafting down a wild river and sleeping in a tent along the bank. Millie's view of a vacation was a resort hotel where she could sit in a lounge chair in the shade and look at nature in the distance while being served elegant food by attentive waiters.

As retirement time approached, Don felt the cumulative years of being trapped in an office. He fantasized more and more about the adventures he wanted to carry out. He had an exercise gym in his home, was in great physical shape and was extremely careful about the kinds of food he ate.

Millie, on the other hand, dreamed that Don's retirement would allow her to quit her full-time job for the school district and that she and Don would be able to take frequent vacation trips to resorts and to see their grandchildren. Millie thought that food was there to eat and physical exercise was something to be avoided.

Now the pressure started to build, because they had not talked about what retirement would mean for them. They had not seriously considered each other's very, very different lifestyles and preferences.

Don had been making a list of all of the things he wanted to do in retirement. His list was almost endless; everything on it was an outdoor adventure. He wanted to hike the total Appalachian Trail ridge from north to south, bike along the West Coast from the Canadian border to Mexico, fish for salmon in Alaska, cross-country ski in Colorado, canoe in the boundary waters of Canada, sail in his own boat in the Caribbean Islands for six months—on and on went his list of adventures.

None of this was interesting to Millie. She couldn't imagine why anyone would want to do such things. Earlier in life she and Don had stopped enjoying their marriage but had tolerated each other. Now their toleration was gone. They frequently fought about what they were going to do when they retired in just fourteen months. Each accused the other: "You always get your way, and you don't care what I want!" A terrible arctic coldness began to settle between the two of them.

It is always a shock when a divorce occurs around retirement. People think, "It's so sad that they made it so many years and then divorced." But whenever the partners change and the marriage relationship is not adjusted, one or both want out. What's the solution? Probably the best answer is effective communication through all the years.

As retirement drew closer, Don began a frantic pace of preparation. He bought a mountain bike and started working out on the hills nearby. He joined a sailing club so that he could improve his skills and be ready to rent a large sailboat in the Caribbean. He started buying backpacking equipment and subscribed to magazines related to his adventures.

When Don was about eight months from retirement, at one of his sailing club meetings he met Jan, who was also taking advanced sailing lessons. Don found himself frequently timing his lessons to coincide with Jan's. She was a forty-two-year-old woman just coming off a divorce and wanting some adventure in life. She was not looking for a man, but she enjoyed Don's friendship because he was always talking about the adventures he was planning.

You guessed it! Before long, Don and Jan were into a full-blown affair. Don told Millie that he wanted a divorce—"because you and I have nothing in common."

Millie was totally taken by surprise. Yes, they had disagreements. Yes, they fought. But she saw the turmoil as a way to work out their differences, and she figured that ultimately they would settle for the same kind of life they had lived previously. They would go to resorts together. Don would have his adventures, and she would stay in the room, enjoying the full amenities offered by the resort.

She was shocked that Don seriously wanted a divorce. She found it hard to believe that he was involved with another woman who he thought was so compatible to him. Suddenly she felt the abandonment. Not only was she losing their long history together, but she felt robbed of all her future retirement plans. Their total assets and retirement benefits were not large enough to support two households.

Don't Let Your Balloon Burst

Abandonment occurs, at whatever stage of life, because of two basic factors. First, the partners are developing, growing and changing in different directions—growing apart, becoming different people than when they were married.

Second, the marriage is not growing as each of the partners change. The marriage remains stuck at an earlier adjustment level that isn't adequate for the new development of one or both of the partners.

It's important to remember that life stages or changes do not actually cause abandonment—*people* make the choices. But these life events can change the balance in a marriage so that abandonment becomes an option. A marriage must continually be adjusted so that both spouses are contented and flourishing.

Some years ago Jim and I were on our way home after leading a marriage enrichment weekend in Northern California. Our daughter Becki and granddaughter Hayden surprised us by coming to the airport, which was near where they lived. They handed me a very pretty balloon for my birthday. I was delighted and carried it with me as we boarded the plane for the one-hour flight back to Southern California.

As the plane kept climbing, my balloon kept getting larger and larger. We were terribly embarrassed as we looked around and noticed other passengers watching this balloon expand far beyond its capacity. Some of them were starting to squint their eyes, expecting an explosion at any moment. Everyone watching the balloon knew it was going to break. The question was when.

As we crossed 20,000 feet on our way to our cruising altitude, the balloon exploded with a horrendous bang. Some passengers had not been paying attention to the balloon saga and thought something had happened to the airplane. They were relieved to know that the frightening sound was just an exploding balloon.

Marriages are like the balloon. They seem to work fine at a certain level of adjustment, but as the environment around the marriage changes, the marriage may blow up. The solution is to continually adjust the marriage. Then the marriage will fit the people who are continuing to grow and evolve.[3]

> This I declare, that he alone is my refuge, my place of safety; he is my God, and I am trusting him. For he rescues you from every trap, and protects you from the fatal plague. He will shield you with his wings! They will shelter you. His faithful promises are your armor. Now you don't need to be afraid of the dark any more, nor fear the dangers of the day; nor dread the plagues of darkness, nor disasters in the morning. (Ps 91:2-6)

— 5 —
The Many
Faces of
Abandonment

IN ADDITION TO COUPLE DEVELOPMENT TIMES AND PREDICTABLE LIFE
stages when a woman could be abandoned, a woman may be
deserted in a variety of ways. Any abandonment by any person
is always painful. But the more a woman loves or needs the other
person, the greater is the intensity of abandonment.

Father Abandonment
A sad chain of events takes place whenever a father, for whatever
reason, abandons his family. The cause may be that the parents'
marriage is so bad it ends in divorce or separation. Or it might
be that the father is dealing with childhood issues that make him
unable to connect with anyone, particularly women. Whatever
the cause, great harm is done to his children.

A father's abandonment affects a woman for all of her life. It
may set her up to be suspicious of men, yet easily manipulated

by them. Her father's abandonment may plant in her the seeds of her own marriage failure.

When a father abandons his daughter, emotionally or physically, the daughter tends to think that it's her fault. She feels, *If I were a better person, my father would love me, want to talk with me and just be with me.*

The abandoned girl not only thinks she's a bad person; she also questions her ability to connect with other men. She reasons, *If I can't manage to connect with my own father, how am I going to connect with a stranger?*

Her deep sense of insecurity caused by her father's abandonment comes into play as she starts to date. She is convinced that she can't please a man, and she's afraid to relate. So when a foolish, sex-craving junior-high boy starts to show an interest in her, she may feel that she finally has a way that enables her to connect to males—sex.

Later she may make a poor choice of a husband, in her desperation to fill up the chasm in her personality caused when her father abandoned her. Girls who have been abandoned are more likely to be later divorced than girls who come from stable, loving homes.[1]

The tragedy is that when a father moves out, he loses the opportunity to give his daughter the affirmation that he ought to give her. He isn't there to tell her that she is special, pretty, intelligent, has a great sensitivity to people's needs and—most of all—that he is grateful that God planned for her to be his daughter.

Marcie is an example of a young woman with a giant hole in her personality called "father hunger." She experienced emotional abandonment when her father was in the home and later physical abandonment when her parents were divorced. She was the younger of two daughters. She always felt she was an inadequate person and that her parents didn't like her.

Marcie's parents had one of those marriages where the partners never really connected emotionally. Yes, they were physically attracted in the early days. Yes, they bore children, did their jobs, attended church, paid the mortgage. But Marcie's parents didn't seem to know how to connect with other people. They each did their own thing and were users rather than givers.

Dad never spent any time talking to either of the girls. Communication was more often in the form of fighting between the parents or their dictatorial commands to the girls.

Marcie was a beautiful girl. She was insightful, with a spontaneous laugh and great sense of humor. She was a fun person to be around. But as you might suspect, she had trouble connecting with men. Yes, she frequently dated because she was so attractive, but unconsciously she didn't let the relationships succeed. She was suspicious of men because of her father's abandonment.

When she was in her early twenties, Marcie became seriously involved with a university student and soon realized that he thought of her as a potential wife. Marcie was very frightened. She found herself drawn to this young man and became sexually involved with him. But she began to pull back. She found reason after reason why the relationship would never work. Unconsciously she was afraid to duplicate her parents' marriage. But even greater was her fear that she might bring a little girl into the world who would feel the same terrible alienation that she felt from her father.

When Marcie's relationship started to fall apart, she also began to gain weight. Suddenly this attractive young woman was thirty pounds overweight. The extra weight was an important protection for her so she wouldn't have to deal with the issue of men.

As we talked, she said, "It would be fun to have a dad that I could trust. Someone who could help me understand men. I'd love to have a dad who could help me buy my first car, even teach me how to drive."

Then Marcie told us of an incident when she and her girlfriend, a university roommate, had taken dinner to an old man whose wife had died. It was Thanksgiving and their church encouraged students who were not going home to think about reaching out to people who might be alone over the holiday. Marcie and her roommate volunteered and were given the name of Mr. Wilcox, a widower in his middle seventies. They made dinner for three and took it to his home. As they chatted, Mr. Wilcox asked questions, learning all that he could about each of them—their schooling, families, boyfriends, hopes and dreams for the future. He also probed a bit into some of their fears.

When the dinner was over, Mr. Wilcox invited them into the living room where he started a fire in the fireplace. He told them about the role of a patriarch in the Old Testament. A patriarch was the leader of the extended family, passing on his wisdom and insight to the generations that would follow and also passing on a blessing to each person.

Mr. Wilcox reached under his chair and pulled out a modern-language edition of the Bible for each of the young women. He said, "Now I want to pray for each of you. I want to pass on to you a blessing, because I feel that in some way your parents have not blessed you as they should have." He reached out his weathered hands and took each one's hand in his.

His prayer for Marcie was very simple and direct, praying for the needs that he sensed in her life that evening. He asked God to compensate for the lack of blessings and affirmation she had experienced from her parents. Marcie wept uncontrollably at the love of this man who hardly knew her and yet gave her a blessing that she so desperately needed.

The world is filled with Marcies who have been abandoned by their fathers. Some have been deserted physically, some emotionally.

There's a tragic correlation between a father's abandonment

and the young woman's becoming sexually active very early, looking for male affection and approval. She may also become involved in drugs or alcohol; she will likely marry an abusive man who, like her father, will abandon her. Or she may never marry because she fears the pain of marriage or is afraid of experiencing the same abandonment process all over again.

The pattern of abandonment sets up a sad cycle. The abandoned young woman may be too insecure, too uninformed or too needy to make an intelligent choice of a mate who is not likely to abandon her. So she marries a man who later abandons her and her children, setting up another generation who will likely continue the cycle of abandonment.

Emotional Abandonment While Married

Typically, when women speak of abandonment they are referring to their husband's physical desertion. Most of the illustrations we are using refer to husbands leaving their wives. What is frequently overlooked, however, is that many people are *emotionally abandoned* while they are yet married. They have all the outward trappings of a marriage, but no emotional connectedness or nourishment exists in the relationship.

This type of abandonment is more difficult to pinpoint because it is a slow-growing process. It's like making a decision about when a business suit is worn out. Is it after so many wearings, or when it doesn't quite hold its shape, or when the cuffs become a little bit threadbare? It's not easy to tell when you should say, "This suit is *finished.*"

Abandonment is a clearcut issue when a man says, "I love another woman" or "I want a divorce." A woman distinctly knows she's being thrown away. But if a marriage seems outwardly normal, it may be hard to tell when the emotional abandonment takes place. The clues are not as clear.

If a man doesn't touch his wife as much as he used to, if he doesn't invite her to go with him as often, if the couple has many widely differing interests or their sexual life becomes less satisfying to both—these and a thousand other expressions of coolness can indicate trouble. But the question is, exactly at what point do you conclude that you are abandoned?

Some years ago, I (Jim) did a door-to-door study of the marriage situation in an affluent Chicago suburb. The sampling fit the national norm—that is, half of the homes had experienced divorce. But what was startling to me was the fact that another twenty-five percent said they would like to be divorced. They stayed together only because of religion, finances, the children or the extended family. They admitted that their marriages were not nourishing. They were not truly marriages in the emotional sense.

Remember the story about how a frog responds to boiling water? If you drop a frog into boiling water, it will immediately jump out. If, however, you put the frog in cold water and gradually heat the water, the frog will not notice the rising temperature and will stay in it until he dies.

Many women reading this book will fall into the category of "emotionally abandoned while yet married." They are somewhat like the frog in the kettle—dying but not realizing it until a husband becomes very cold, indifferent or hostile. We want to encourage you to have hope for yourself and for your marriage. You'll be able to apply many of the concepts in this book to help revitalize your marriage.

Abandonment by Death

Another type of "abandonment" happens when a husband dies. Society validates only one type of reaction from the widow. She is to be grief-stricken, devastated at the loss of her husband. But in addition, she is to get over all of those feelings in about three weeks.

Many widows feel as if their husband has abandoned them

through death. Women who are divorced sometimes feel resentful toward widows. "They have it easy," some divorcées say of widows. "People feel sorry for them and even bring in casseroles." But a widow experiences many of the same feelings as a divorced woman. She may have raging surges of shock, numbness, panic, anger, withdrawal, a desire to punish, a sad feeling, depression, even despair or suicidal thoughts. She may also experience fear, shame, guilt, a lowered self-image and a loss of coping skills. Many of these feelings are kept submerged by the woman who has been widowed. Yet in moments of honesty, many widows admit that they've had to work through very intense reactions.

One of the most common feelings when a husband dies is anger at him for dying. Marge blurted out to us, "Why was Keith so stubborn? He knew he needed to have nitroglycerin pills near him. Why didn't he just admit his need and have pills in various places around the house? No! No! He had to keep the pills downstairs in the kitchen cupboard. And every time he had a pain in the night he was too proud to wake me up. He'd get up and go downstairs himself to take a pill. Why couldn't he have just kept some pills at his bedside? Why couldn't he have shaken me and said, 'I'm having another spell'?

"It's a terrible, terrible thing to hear a crash and know your husband has fallen. I got up and ran downstairs as fast as I could and found Keith slumped in the hallway. He hadn't made it to the kitchen cupboard. He was unconscious. I ran to the kitchen and tried to get a pill into his mouth, but it was too late.

"I felt horrible, waiting forever and ever for the ambulance to come. When the paramedics arrived, they worked on him in the house. Then he was on a stretcher and out our front door. The ambulance lights were flashing round and round our whole neighborhood. Porch lights came on—the neighbors wondered why the ambulance was there. But I was numb with shock.

"I felt I was in a terrible dream as we went to the emergency room. I watched helplessly as they tried to revive him. His body convulsed again and again. But no response. He was dead.

"What do I do with all of these feelings?" Marge asked us. "I'm so angry at Keith for being stubborn. Why are men so arrogant—so pigheaded?" Then she paused for a long time and finally said, "I feel ashamed for even having those feelings.

"So now I'm not only dealing with all of my anger and rage, but I'm also dealing with shame and guilt. How can I be angry at a good man like Keith? But he left me! I don't know anything about our finances! And now I've got this big house to take care of. He dumped it all in my lap. He just abandoned me!"

Somehow society must learn that there's more to death than just a funeral service and more to recovery than a few weeks of grieving. It takes a minimum of a year to go through all the events such as anniversaries, birthdays and holidays. Each of the special times must be experienced without the spouse before recovery can realistically be accomplished. It's not only the moment of dying that needs to be healed—so do the ten thousand moments of remembering.

A widow must not allow herself to get stuck in the pain of the death abandonment. The recovery process we will discuss later in the book applies also to the widow and will help her move on past her grief.

The potential for a woman's being abandoned in some form sometime during her life is very great. Later in the book we'll talk more about prevention of abandonment and preparation in case of abandonment.

I would have died unless the Lord had helped me. I screamed, "I'm slipping, Lord!" and he was kind and saved me. Lord, when doubts fill my mind, when my heart is in turmoil, quiet me and give me renewed hope and cheer. (Ps 94:17-19)

— 6 —

Why a Woman Becomes Disposable

*R*ECENTLY I (JIM) WAS HANGING OUT WITH A GROUP OF MEN BETWEEN sessions at a men's conference. I asked them to tell me their feelings about women. "What do you like about women—why are they important in your life?" They listed things such as companionship, insights, stability, spirituality, mothering and sex. The whole group gave an embarrassed laugh at the word *sex*.

Then I asked, "What do you think a woman could do, say or act like that would irritate a man to the point of leaving her?"

The men were quiet until I assured them they didn't have to talk about their own marriages but could discuss husbands and wives in general. Then the comments began to pour out. Before long they got very intense and personal: "What really irritates *me* is . . . " or "I don't see things changing much in my wife's attitude about . . . "

In this chapter we have distilled the main concerns we heard expressed by this group, along with those of thousands of other men from other conferences, counseling sessions, and letter and phone contacts.

Women who become disposable tend to have some common characteristics. Again, it's important to remember at this point that we're not discussing *what is right or wrong*, nor are we looking at marriage commitments, vows and the role of a good husband; we're simply saying this is *what is*.

At the same time that we are talking about *what is*, we must be careful not to beat up on the woman who has already been smashed by abandonment. Our purpose in this chapter is not to lay guilt or to get you to ask, "What if I were sexier, thinner, smarter, shorter, taller, richer"—or on and on with the second guesses. Nor is the focus here a marital postmortem—you will do that later. Here we want to face some of the hard facts of *what is*.

His Changing Needs

The confusing question that many women wrestle with is, "If I am continuing to do things the same way as I've done them all of our married life, why has my husband decided that I no longer meet his needs?"

One reason is that *he is changing*. Parts of his personality may be finally awakening. As we saw earlier, the life cycle development of a husband causes his needs to continually change. In his twenties he may have been very task-oriented, but as he crosses forty he may become more person-oriented. He wants to look up old college friends. He is thinking again about the good old days. He wants to recapture his youth. He also becomes more reflective, asking questions about the purpose of life. He begins to see the importance of connecting with people at a feeling level. The years have made him more sensitive, even though he is still under career pressure and does not have much free time.

If a wife doesn't understand the changes in her husband and adjust accordingly, he will conclude that she doesn't meet his needs. Obviously, the reverse holds true as well! If a husband isn't meeting his wife's needs, she will feel misunderstood and unloved.

Men look at life differently at different ages. Teenagers and young adults are future-oriented, while mid-life men are "now"-oriented. Young adults console themselves with imperfections of people and life in general by saying, "When I get older, life will be different." But as people move across each of the five-year time lines, an automatic sense of calculation takes place as they ask, "How am I doing? Am I contented with what's happening in my life?" Often, things don't seem to be getting better.

A wife may be doing things exactly as she was during the first fifteen years of their marriage. She may not realize that her husband is in panic because he is crossing one of those five-year lines. His quiet personal assessment is that life is not what he planned it to be. In particular, his relationship with his wife is not as fulfilling as he imagined—and he has given up hope that she will ever understand him.

As a result, he begins to toy with the idea—in the "playground of his mind"—that maybe he ought to leave his wife. *After all, divorce can't be that bad,* he says to himself. *My parents went through it, and my wife's parents also. Maybe it's true that in our culture it's no longer realistic to expect one marriage to last a lifetime. I've certainly met a lot of other women more attractive than my wife—and some of them seem to better understand what I want out of life.*

These life changes do not *cause* a man to abandon his wife. He could also choose to talk to his wife about how he is changing. Or his wife could be more in tune with her husband and notice that he is changing. They could choose to communicate and adjust, rather than simply blame each other.

The Bible speaks plainly about what is likely to happen: "Remember, when someone wants to do wrong it is never God who is tempting him, for God never wants to do wrong and never tempts anyone else to do it. Temptation is the pull of man's own evil thoughts and wishes. These evil thoughts lead to evil actions and afterwards to the death penalty from God. So don't be misled" (Jas 1:13-16).

It's predictable: if a husband and wife are not meeting each other's needs, one or the other may allow his or her mind to play with thoughts of greener pastures. This may ultimately lead to abandoning the relationship.

A Mother Instead of a Lover

If a couple marries in the late teens or early twenties, the woman is often more mature and sometimes more responsible than the man. In fact, that's one of the qualities that attracts a man to a woman—her stability. As the couple ages, however, and the husband picks up more skills and maturity, he doesn't need the "mothering" of his wife as much as he did at the beginning.

At the same time, with the coming of children the wife's mothering qualities blossom to their fullest capacity. Sometimes you'll hear a woman joking that she has four children, three in grade school and one in his early thirties.

The tired wife, consumed with the demands of child-rearing and perhaps employment as well, may stop taking romantic initiative and seem less responsive. She takes good care of her husband and kids—but by the time he crosses the forty-year mark, her husband is wanting something very different from a second mother. In such a case, abandonment typically takes place in the form of an affair. He may look for someone who will relate to him as a lover instead of a mother.

Again, the changes didn't *cause* the abandonment; both spouses made choices along the way that had a sad effect.

Weight Gain or Loss

Men are very visual. When a man decides to date a particular woman, he is probably physically attracted to her first. Men and women commonly speak about a man being a "leg man" or a "breast man." This is not a reference to whether he wants light or dark meat when he orders Kentucky Fried Chicken! It means that men carry a visual image of their ideal woman with a particular focus on certain body parts.

Men don't select a wife *only* on the basis of physical characteristics, but a woman's appearance is very important to a man. Yes, we hope he is looking for intelligence, companionship, education, spirituality and a lot of other things. But if she has all of those characteristics and her body doesn't match his mental image, he's likely to keep looking.

Now a problem arises. As people age, body weight moves from limbs to torso. Ears get larger, noses grow longer, and the space between the bottom of the nose and the bottom of the chin gets longer too. The body continues to change; everything sags, and most people gain weight.

If those changes are gradual, the couple has time to adjust. If, however, a sudden weight gain or weight loss takes place, the husband may find himself looking at an entirely different person. And he may find uncomfortable thoughts dancing around the playground of his mind. He may conclude that if he chose a wife again, he would not choose this woman.

Ideally, commitment will have grown in the marriage relationship so that when bodily changes do occur because of aging, stress or illness, the two will be able to rise above visual reality as they work together on communication and commitment.

But remember, in this section of the book we are not dealing with *what ought to be* but *what is*. The *what is* of life is that if a wife is not meeting her husband's needs, if she is more of a mother than a lover, and if she has had drastic physical changes since marriage, the possibility of abandonment is increased.

The wife is not causing the abandonment! The husband still has a choice. The mature husband will not walk out over these issues; neither will the mature wife deliberately allow these issues to irritate.

Stressed Out and Nasty

During the dating years, couples have high energy and low responsibility. They don't realize it at the time, but over the next ten to twenty years their stress level is going to rise sharply, with a vast increase in responsibilities.

When the young couple is first married, a lot of emotional energy is spent on adjusting to each other and trying to create a *we* out of the two *I*'s. When a child comes along, they may find themselves overwhelmed with continued marriage adjustments, pressure to succeed in their careers and the twenty-four-hours-a-day care for this infant.

Before the child is two years old, the wife may be pregnant again, and all of the unresolved adjustments are carried into the new nine months of pregnancy. The second child is born, and the couple who originally had two interpersonal relationships— that is, his relationship to her and hers to him—now find that their family has twelve interpersonal relationships to keep running smoothly.

Now add to the mix the possibility of PMS (premenstrual syndrome). For some women, their hormonal level dips some days before their monthly period. This may cause a woman to have more physical fatigue and a lower stress capacity. In addition, some women wrestle with a chronic physical problem such as hypoglycemia (low blood sugar) that causes fatigue and a lowered ability to cope with life.

If she tries to be a superwoman—to carry a full career, full mothering responsibilities, and full community and church involvement, *and* to be a full-time lover—she may find herself stressed beyond the breaking point. Tragically, she may start lashing out and become nasty, nasty, nasty.

The husband has a choice in all of these events. He can either share the load in order to reduce the pressure or blame his wife and become nasty too. The result could be a home out of control and with a free flow of negative remarks so that the husband will say, "I want out." He may begin to rationalize, "It's bad for the children to hear us fighting all the time. We are destroying each other."

Again, we're looking at *what is*, not *what should be*. What should be is that the husband and wife will face the growing stress and see that the nasty and perhaps violent environment is not because the wife is inherently bad—she is overstressed. The pressures have outstripped her capacity to cope with life. Life pressures need to be adjusted so their marriage—and each of them—can survive. If a husband doesn't see that, he may run from the marriage simply to escape the hostile environment.

Sexual Abuse in Childhood

Commonly, a woman will not share about sexual abuse that may have occurred in her childhood. She thinks it is not important to tell this while she is dating her potential husband. Or she may deliberately withhold this information out of fear that she might lose this guy if he learns how sick her family was.

In addition, many women have totally blocked out the fact they were sexually abused or molested by a trusted adult—a father, grandfather or uncle. The little girl may have been given little bribes or terrible warnings when these unspeakable acts took place so that she unconsciously willed herself to forget. The child has little emotional power and few resources to fight back against the trusted adult. Therefore, she suffers the molestation and buries it deep in her psyche, not even realizing it is there.

When the young woman gets married and establishes her own home, she has a feeling of being more in charge of her life and destiny. Now her unconscious mind may start to release bits and pieces of memory flashes about the terrible deeds.

In addition, the coming of children changes her role in life. As a parent, she gains new insights into the evil deeds she had to endure as a child. She grows to understand why she is so protective of her children. Her husband may be surprised she is so paranoid, as he sees it, about sexual abuse.

As her unconscious psyche is freer, and as she gains more control of life, she begins to remember the awfulness of the atrocious acts. Suddenly she is lashing out with anger and frustration. She wants to control everything around her. She wants to protect her children. She's not sure if she can trust her husband; she may, for a while, totally withdraw from sexual intercourse.

The uninformed husband may feel he has done something wrong. Even his wife's assurances that this is not his fault don't help him. Finally, she may be able to tell him that her agonizing problems are related to childhood sexual abuse by a trusted adult.

The "twentysomething" husband is in the black-and-white era of his life. To him this is simply a task to be resolved. He tells her, "Forget about it. That happened a long time ago. Let's just go on and live our lives now. Don't let this tear us up."

But, you see, she has tried all her life to "forget it." It hasn't worked. The pain is still bubbling out. Forgetting it did not eliminate the pain; it only delayed it. The husband may not understand his wife's problem, and he may feel that she is deliberately prolonging the situation, intentionally not forgetting it.

Instead, a woman needs her husband's support. He will need to be her strong encourager during her restoration, which may be a lengthy process. She will probably require in-depth counseling as God walks with her back into those terrible events and heals the pain of that sin committed against her. A woman needs her husband's encouragement while she works through the painful memories and her agonizing grieving. She also needs his support for the confrontation and eventual forgiveness of the guilty one.

The husband can be a great ally in the process of confronting the perpetrator and encouraging the healing process. Or he can abandon his wife, hoping to find some woman who has not had these kinds of problems. (He may not realize that massive numbers of women have been sexually molested before they're eighteen years of age. The likelihood of his finding another person untouched by this evil is remote.)

Whether we like it or not, one of the characteristics we see in abandonment is the connection to the husband's inability or unwillingness to handle the effects of childhood sexual abuse on his wife.

Power and Money

When a couple is first married, they generally establish unspoken guidelines about money and power. Since both of them probably worked before they were married, it's often assumed that the wife will continue to work. If a baby comes along, she can take off a couple of weeks and then they will simply get a baby sitter—right! They think of a child as getting a new puppy. Yes, you have to spend a little time training it at the beginning, but, essentially, you just feed the pup and he's on his own.

But, surprise, surprise, the child takes twenty-four hours a day. The parents can't find anyone to baby-sit for more than a couple of hours, and suddenly the wife is elected to be a full-time stay-at-home mom.

A gigantic earthquake has just taken place regarding money and power. To most people, money is power. Whoever earns the money has the power.

Dwayne and Mary Lou are a good example. Dwayne earns one hundred percent of the family income. He thinks of it as his income, not the family's. He doesn't see that Mary Lou is an equal partner or that her contribution as a homemaker and mother is worth thousands of dollars.

He is the financial dictator—the controller with money power. "I'll give you $250 of my $780 weekly paycheck. That should cover our food, clothes for you and the kids, and anything else that you need for the house. I'll take care of the mortgage, car payments and maintenance, and I'll pay the medical insurance." They are not deciding together how they should spend their money. Rather, Dwayne thinks of himself as a benevolent king who gives his slaves a dollar dole.

Since the money is really his, Dwayne thinks, he has no problem buying anything he wants without asking his wife. He picks up a new leather jacket and $125 running shoes. When he gets a raise at work, Mary Lou doesn't get more. Instead he has more money to buy a better car, improve the stereo, get a bigger TV screen for weekend football games and join a health spa for some serious bodybuilding.

The focus is on Dwayne's needs and desires. Earning the money is power for him. Mary Lou questions, *Why does he get to spend money for whatever he wants?* But she is afraid to say anything because she too has bought into the idea that "whoever earns the money owns the money." Mary Lou accepts Dwayne's financial controlling and allows herself to be driven deeper and deeper into resentment. She is starting to hate marriage—and Dwayne. *Why does it have to be this way?* she asks.

Not only is Mary Lou beginning to dislike marriage, but Dwayne is beginning to devalue her in his mind. He increasingly finds the women at work stimulating and intriguing. At this point, Dwayne is skating on very thin ice.

The other side of the money/power issue is if the wife earns more money than her husband. A number of studies have shown that when the wife earns considerably more than her husband, he feels powerless. At first, the husband views his wife's additional salary or large inheritance very positively. *Wow, just think of all the great things we can do with this extra money.* But suddenly he realizes that she is possessive of "her money," and the decision-making power is not his alone. An insecure man is threatened and may try to escape the threat by abandoning the marriage.

Uneven Growth

Another typical characteristic of a woman who is abandoned is that she either outgrows her husband or doesn't keep up with his growth. It's unfortunate that this factor should cause estrangement, but it can.

Martha and Jack were high-school sweethearts. They both got jobs after high school and married a year later. Ten years into their marriage, Martha joined a neighborhood Bible study group. Suddenly religion was not simply something to do only on Sunday. It became very personal to Martha. She studied the Bible every day, along with other books that were suggested by the study group.

A year and a half later, she was invited to go for group leadership training at a regional retreat center. Soon she was leading her own group and giving basic training to other area leaders. Their church noticed Martha's leadership in the community Bible study and asked if she would be willing to serve in a leadership capacity for the church. Before long, Martha was serving on several different committees within the church and eventually was nominated for the major leadership board.

By now, Martha and Jack had been married about fifteen years. At first, Jack ignored Martha's involvement in the study group, thinking it was just women's stuff. But as Martha gained more prominence in the community and the church, Jack felt left out. He started finding reasons to avoid going to church or to be with Martha's friends. A growing vacuum crept into their marriage relationship, because Jack didn't want to talk about Martha's leadership interests, which were involving more and more of her time.

As their relationship continued to deteriorate, they each made the choice to ignore the growing separation. Neither of them acknowledged the problem. Instead of their talking and growing together, Jack found a friend. One day over coffee at work he shared with a lonely female employee about how much Martha was involved in all of her church activities. It took only a few short steps for two needy people to find themselves involved in an emotional and physical affair.

Fortunately, Martha realized what was happening. She and Jack talked very frankly about their marriage situation. As a result, Martha backed off on some of her leadership duties, and Jack started to work at his own personal growth, which led to his appreciating the special leadership skills of his wife. Together they also began doing more of the outdoor activities that had been so much a part of their early married life.

In other marriages, a man may excuse himself for abandoning his wife not because she is growing too fast but because she is not growing at all. Typically, this happens when the husband has frequent exposure to bright, assertive women. If, by contrast, he sees his wife as *only* a wife and mother who talks *only* about the children's activities, a growing distance may develop between the two of them.

The comparison may become visible to the husband when they are at a company function and he is embarrassed to introduce his wife to the rising young females in the organization He suddenly may feel that he has more in common with the career women than with his wife and family. Sadly, he may find himself on the slippery path toward abandonment.

Is It the Woman's Fault?

All of these characteristics we've described are really just snap-shots of what the woman looks like or how she is behaving and thinking at the time her husband begins to consider leaving her. Many people might conclude that the woman is at fault for the abandonment taking place. That might be the case in some instances, but generally neither the wife nor the husband is directly to blame—it's just that the equilibrium within the marriage has been thrown off. Blame may be charged if, during the uneasiness in the marriage, one or both of them make a bad choice that destroys the marriage. Both could have chosen to communicate and rebuild instead of ignoring the problem or escaping.

When the couple first decided to marry, they each thought of the other as the best possible mate. They assessed many other people and determined that this one person best met their needs.

But now the situation has changed. Aging, awareness of childhood sexual abuse, the birth of children, the shift in the money/power relationship, or all of these together have given each of them a different view of themselves and of each other. None of these things by itself is the culprit.

Change is the culprit. Change, unfortunately, can become the disturbance that triggers abandonment. Or the same change can bring about new growth, love and deeper commitment.

Too Much of a Good Thing

Life has meaning only as we keep growing and changing. It is change that gives us new insights and capacities. Change should be a positive stimulation and keep us and our marriage from being boring, boring, boring.

On the other hand, we need stability and dependability to give us the security that is so crucial for our lives. *A good marriage is a combination of stability and change.* Both of these are necessary to help us live a productive and happy life.

The problem comes when there is either too much change or too much stability. People become uncomfortable. They typically run away from pain and move toward pleasure. If there is too much stability or change, couples may become uneasy—and one may want out. However, healthy people try to help each other adjust. They choose to talk—not fix blame or run.

We must recognize that the degree of change in a marriage is not the only factor behind an abandonment. And it is not a valid reason for one partner to leave the marriage. Yet it's important to understand the part each factor plays.

When it's the man who walks out, the woman may conclude that change brought about by her rapid educational or spiritual growth played a part. But she may ultimately decide that that very change was the best thing that happened in her life. She may not be willing to give up the personal growth she has achieved, even to keep her marriage—especially not to keep a husband who is physically abusive or mentally controlling.

Mildred was such a woman. We met her when she was serving as a waitress. She liked her job, but we could tell she was a sad woman. Her sadness was visible as she served us and other people.

Some years passed before we saw her again. By then she was a different person, exuding enthusiasm and confidence. She told us she had gone to school to get training as a nurse. She had made high grades and was now employed in a position with a great deal of responsibility as a department head.

She said, "My ex-husband would flip if he could see how capable I am. He always told me I was dumb and I couldn't do anything right. I can't tell you how many times he yelled insults as he whacked me around in front of our children."

Mildred continued, "It was my kids who urged me to go to school so I could earn a decent wage. When my husband saw that I was no longer going to cower before him, he got furious and left."

This "dumb, incompetent" woman (in her ex-husband's eyes) has supported herself and her children for five years now. "I love my work and am highly respected. I wouldn't go back to the old days for anything "

In my distress I prayed to the Lord and he answered me and rescued me. He is for me! How can I be afraid? What can mere man do to me? The Lord is on my side, he will help me. . . . It is better to trust the Lord than to put confidence in men. (Ps 118:5-8)

—Part Three—

The Recovery Process

I (Jim) have enjoyed cooking for much of my adult life. I'm the kind of cook who is not contented with the standard recipe. When I look at a recipe, I constantly ask myself, *What can I do to make it better?*

For example, one of my recent creations is to take a standard apple pie recipe, add about one-fourth more apples, my secret spices, then tapioca for thickening. Here's the real secret: after I've put half the pie mixture into the deep, pastry-lined pie dish, I add a layer of frozen red raspberries. On top of the raspberries I sprinkle chopped nuts. Finally I put the rest of the apple mixture on top, add the crust, and bake it for about an hour. There you have it! A wonderful pie that I call Jim's Apple Raspberry Nut Pie.

But let me also tell you about one of my catastrophes. I was in a hurry to get the pie baked, so I decided to make just a plain apple pie. In order to save time, I didn't peel the apples. I put all of the stuff together, spread it in the pie plate, put on the top crust and stuck it in the oven.

As I started to clean up, I noticed that I hadn't put any thickening into the pie mixture. It was going to be one soupy mess. So I quickly pulled the pie out of the oven. By now the top crust was warm and had gotten to that soft, sticky state. I knew I couldn't lift the crust off to put in the thickening, so I just cut holes in the top of the pie and poked flour down through the holes, hoping that it might still do its job.

Those of you who are cooks know what happened. It came out to be a runny mess with blobs of flour here and there just under the top crust! The problem wasn't that I had forgotten the ingredients; it was that I hadn't mixed in the flour for thickening at the right stage of the process.

Exactly the same thing is true when you're trying to bounce back after being dumped by your mate. If you do things out of order, you're going to end up in a mess. For example, don't throw yourself into new career training or a new relationship just after you've learned that your mate has abandoned you. If you fail to do the necessary grieving and to feel your pain, you will prolong your recovery. The decisions you make in your desperate attempt to fix the situation will probably be wrong.

In the following chapters we are going to look at three distinct stages that people go through before they can begin to rebuild after being discarded. Stage one is shock, which we'll talk about in chapter seven. Stage two is working to save the relationship (chapter eight). When the marriage cannot be saved, stage three is facing the abandonment, making it all the way through the pain to acceptance (chapter nine). After acceptance is finally arrived at, the next task is reconstruction, encompassing several issues in an abandoned woman's life (chapters ten through fourteen).

As we launch into the recovery process, let's consider the *feelings* and the *tasks* you should handle during each stage. By dealing with the feelings for that one stage only, and by keeping your focus limited to your primary task, your recovery will be accelerated—and with less guilt.

Following is a simplified list of what your *feelings* and your *tasks* should be in each stage. Remember that you will not be able to perfectly follow this chart—your emotions will bounce around among the stages. That's okay—you're normal.

Stage One—Shock

☐ *Feelings:* Anger, loneliness, depression, indignation, sadness, rage, failure, plus many more related to being abandoned.

☐ *Tasks:* Feel your feelings. Write them out. Share them with a few close friends, a counselor and God. Allow no self-blame at this stage.

Stage Two—Restoration

☐ *Feelings:* Let your heart feel the painful questions, What part did I have in the breakup? Can I honestly give up on this marriage without trying my very best to restore it? What steps should I take now?

☐ *Tasks:* Take responsibility only for yourself. Don't accept blame for your husband's part in the marriage failure. Focus on controlling and stabilizing yourself. You can't control your husband, but you can control yourself. Blaming your husband, focusing on the past and beating up on yourself will be counter-productive. We will coach you on positive ways to give your best shot at trying to restore your marriage.

Stage Three—Acceptance

☐ *Feelings:* Affirm yourself for doing your best. Trust God to work to heal the past and give you a future of hope.

☐ *Tasks:* Release your past marriage and your former husband to God. Redirect your thoughts away from past pain to your future.

Again, remember that you are unique. You probably will not feel and do things exactly as this outline says. Its purpose is to reduce guilt and to help you know what is common to many women in your situation. Treat yourself with tenderness; don't put unrealistic expectations on yourself.

— 7 —

Shock

*R*EMEMBER ANN FROM THE FIRST PART OF THE BOOK? SHE SHARED with us the intensity of her shock and anger, her feeling of wanting to be away from everyone. She also shared her desire to punish Bob. At the same time, she felt sadness, fear and a guilty feeling that something must be wrong with her. In sorting out your own confused emotions, you may want to take some of the same steps we advised Ann to take.

What to Do
Feel your feelings. When Ann first talked to us, soon after Bob's abandonment, her initial reaction was one of denial. One moment she was half-expecting that he would return any day; minutes later she was in tears at remembering Bob's statement that he was leaving and involved with another woman. Then she would bravely state, "I think he'll realize pretty soon that he

doesn't really want to toss away his family. He'll be back."

The first temptation of the abandoned woman is to deny that abandonment is happening and to hide her true feelings. She acts as if denial will change the reality.

We encouraged Ann to feel her pain, to realize that every one of the emotions that had surged through her in those first moments, and every moment since then, was a normal sensation. "In fact," we told Ann, "it would be abnormal *not* to feel those emotions."

Since Ann was from a Christian background, she also needed to understand that God was not shocked by her emotions. Nor was she a spiritual failure because she felt these feelings.

Make slips of paper. One of the homework assignments we gave Ann was to read a psalm from the Bible each day and to list emotions that were expressed or implied by the writer. The psalmist would come to God, outline his list of woes, then shift from painful emotions to a deep confidence in God. Just as the psalmists were real with their emotions, so the abandoned woman doesn't need to be afraid of God or the emotions that he has created in her.

Ann began keeping a written log of her feelings as she read the Bible—a separate piece of paper for each of her emotions related to Bob and the situation. The next time we saw her she showed us her slips of paper. Across the top of each slip she had written a feeling, such as anger. Then in a few sentences, with as much emotion as possible, she had written out the specific way she was experiencing that feeling. On the slip titled ANGER, for example, were these words: "I'm angry that Bob is spending money on Jennifer that should be used for our kids."

Transferring her feelings to written form was important for Ann. Later in the healing process, these slips of paper became part of a ritual to help her recover from Bob's abandonment.

Be poised, not pathetic. Ann was able to objectify her problem.

86

It's very different to say, *I am a person and I have this problem* from saying, *I am a problem, and I've lost my personhood.*

At stage one—shock—it's difficult not to become entwined with the problem to such a degree that you think of *yourself* as the problem. The goal is to be a poised person who says to herself, *I am a person who has a problem, but I'm going to work toward a solution.* You can maintain your dignity as a person and as a woman, refusing to accept the negative messages that the circumstances may seem to be giving you ("you're inadequate; you're sexually deficient; you're dumb"), realizing that these are false messages.

Yes, it's okay to say, *I'm being smashed by all of these emotions. These are my feelings; these are my reactions.* But you must follow that by saying, *Nevertheless, I am going to survive; I am going to work through this problem.*

Allow for the passage of time. At first, time seems to be your enemy. It's going so slowly and nothing seems to be getting any better. In fact, as we saw in Ann's life during the early days, time seemed to be her adversary as it uncovered more and more problems.

But after a while, time will become your friend. Each day will become a new day in the recovery process. You will gain greater stability. You will understand yourself better. Your husband's abandonment will become a powerful tool for your own growth. Your deeper understanding of yourself and other people will make you a more effective person and will help your friendships grow. You'll also have a greater capacity to help other people struggling with a variety of life's stresses.

What Not to Do
Don't deny. In Ann's situation, she wasn't deliberately denying that Bob was abandoning her. The shock numbed and overwhelmed her so that she couldn't speak when Bob left the house

that evening. Her initial defense was to hope, to imagine, that he would return soon and this awful experience would be over.

Some women, however, continue the denial to themselves and to other people even after the initial shock wears off. Frequently, a woman is embarrassed because of the family's position in the community. She tries to cover up any hint that something is wrong: "He's just on a business trip" or "He's spending long hours at the office."

This is a very tricky, delicate time. Ann didn't want to deny telling the truth to herself or her close friends. On the other hand, she didn't want to make a public announcement that Bob had abandoned her and run off with Jennifer. She continued to face reality with herself, with us, with her lawyer and with two other trusted friends. These special friends knew the whole truth and were able to give her balanced support. They also kept Ann's situation confidential.

Don't beat up on yourself. Again, it's easy in the first days of abandonment to punish yourself. *If only I had been more sensitive, more understanding of his work pressures. If only I had been more sexy. If only, if only, if only.*

Later you will need to go through this process of discovering your part in the abandonment, but for now these "if onlys" are the same as standing in front of the mirror and beating yourself in the face with your own fists. Don't beat up on yourself. If you need to tell yourself something, say, *I'm not exactly sure why all of this has happened, but I will work it out, with God's help.*

Don't "catastrophize." Years ago we read an amusing story about a man who had a flat tire on a country road. When he opened his trunk, he found that he had no jack to raise the car and put on the spare tire. Seeing a farmhouse about half a mile away, he decided to walk there and ask if he could borrow a jack.

On the way he started imagining nervously what the farmer

might say to him and how he would respond:

He imagined himself knocking on the door several times. Finally a farmer opened the door; he seemed annoyed and said in an angry voice, "What do you want?"

The stranded motorist said, "Well, I have a flat tire and I don't have my jack."

Farmer: "Why don't you have a jack?"

Motorist: "Well, I was rotating the tires on my car one day, and I guess I just forgot to put the jack back in the trunk."

Farmer: "Well, that shouldn't be my problem. You were so stupid that you failed to put your jack back in the trunk. That's your problem! No, I *won't* loan you my jack."

About this time the stranded motorist actually arrived at the front door and knocked. A farmer came to the door with a big smile on his face and said, "What can I do for you?"

But by this time, the motorist was so irate at what he had *imagined* the farmer would say that he blurted out, "I don't want your jack anyway!" Then he spun around and walked back to his car empty-handed.

The abandoned woman must not allow herself to overplay her situation. She must not exaggerate what is happening. Yes, it's very bad, but don't let your mind run away with you.

"Just deal with the facts," we told Ann. "It's bad enough that Bob has abandoned you and that he is attracted to Jennifer—but that's all you really know."

In those first hours and days, Ann had imagined all kinds of things. She decided that Bob probably had had dozens of previous affairs and that all of those women were more beautiful and sexually alluring than she was. She also imagined that Bob had secret bank accounts and had siphoned off thousands of dollars into these accounts to be used for entertaining the other women.

Her mind played games, driving her wild. She painted pictures of Bob and Jennifer away at a retreat hotel. She could see them eating dinner together and then walking in the moonlight. She became frantic as her mind drew scenes of Jennifer undressing in front of Bob and all of the ways he was touching her. Then she imagined the two of them in bed in a passionate sexual embrace.

When Ann shared with us the extent of her mental images, we reminded her that she needed to force her mind to deal only with known facts—not with fantasy. The Bible says the devil "prowls around like a hungry, roaring lion, looking for some victim to tear apart" (1 Pet 5:8). Wild, anxious exaggeration is not God trying to help you; it is demonic activity trying to destroy you. You can choose to keep away from the enemy's influence by sticking with the facts.

Typically, the other woman is not a stunningly attractive person, but rather someone who reaches out with understanding to the man in stress. Bob had changed. Like many men, he so much needed a new depth of care and understanding that he was willing to abandon his wife, family—everything, if necessary—as he wrestled with the new awakenings in his personality. He was not willing to see that Ann could understand his changes and meet his needs now as she had done all through their marriage.

Don't overreact. Exaggeration magnifies imagined problems into catastrophes. Overreaction is the action that easily follows on the heels of exaggeration, because the bad things that we imagine seem to be actually happening. Therefore, we start to make abrupt life changes based on these distortions.

Ann told us some of the sudden changes that she considered in those early days after Bob had abandoned her. In her anger and hurt, she thought of many actions that were very unlike her.

One evening she dressed in her sexiest clothes and went into a singles bar in a nearby suburb. She ordered wine, even though she never drank. She intentionally perched on the bar stool sideways, allowing her legs to be clearly visible beneath her short, tight skirt. Soon men started to hit on her, and she started flirting back. After about half an hour, one of the guys suggested that they go to his place.

Then Ann panicked! She said, "I felt as if I'd been hit with a cold, wet towel. His invitation jolted me into reality. I didn't want to be in that bar. I didn't want to drink. I didn't want to go to bed with some strange man. I was just furious with Bob and trying to punish him. I was trying to make him jealous—but he wasn't there to see me. I was really only punishing myself."

So, part of this "don't do" list is to not overreact and make abrupt changes in your life. It is crucial that you keep up your normal routine as much as possible. Don't change jobs, don't break off with your friends, don't stop going to church, work or social gatherings. Don't change the locks on the doors or remove your husband's name from your savings and checking accounts. Don't lose all sense of stability.

We do want to caution that keeping things as normal as possible does not mean that you should continue to be physically abused by your husband, if that is going on. In such a case, you may need to change the locks or take other precautions. Nor do we suggest that a husband should be allowed to drain your joint bank account as he trades the family's financial security for a fling with his new girlfriend. If there is evidence of such behavior, you may need to rearrange finances, perhaps moving some money into a bank account in your name only. Be in touch with a lawyer early to protect yourself and your children.

Don't be punitive. It's easy for a chain reaction of feelings, followed by behaviors, to take place once we allow exaggerating and overreacting to set in. If Ann had allowed herself to believe all that she imagined about Bob and Jennifer, it would have been easy for her to want revenge. She might even have delighted in the thoughts of what she could do to get even.

In fact, Ann did tell us some of her fantasies about punishing Bob: ripping out the seats of all his suit pants; smearing lipstick into the shoulders of his jackets; running an ice pick into his tires when his car was parked at Jennifer's.

She also thought of ways to sabotage him at work. She knew how strict the boss was about office love affairs, so she plotted different ways to arrange for both Bob and Jennifer to lose their jobs. She thought too about taking out large cash advances against all the credit cards, plus charging thousands of dollars in stores that don't use electronic verification. Then Bob would have massive overdrafts in both the charge card accounts and the store accounts.

She also thought about getting a line of credit, in her name only, against the equity in the house. Since the house was almost paid off, it would be a quick way to strip Bob of his wealth. But Ann was just overreacting in her mind. She wasn't even sure she could do some of these things legally, and she knew she couldn't do them in good conscience.

Don't be confrontive. Imagine two kids playing in a sandbox. They start to fight over a toy, and one of them hits the other. The child who is hit swings back with reflex action, and soon they are hard at it in a crying and hitting match. The temptation when a woman has been abandoned is to bash back: *It's time to get even. I'm going to tell him off. I need to confront him and read the riot act.*

"But," we said to Ann, "if you start to tell Bob off, you'll find yourself not only focusing on this immediate abandonment, but also dragging up every past issue of married life. You'll rehearse all the problems you've ever had with his brothers, sisters and parents, and all the ways he has mistreated the children. The list will go on and on.

"This is not the time to confront him. This is the time to let the dust settle. During the shock stage, your confrontation will most likely be overreaction. If you overreact, you won't bring healing, you'll just be throwing dust into the air. For now, keep your conversations with Bob focused on the family needs and the fact that you still love him. Later you'll be able to talk rationally about this problem and to directly confront him about the bad choice he has made by leaving you and the family."

It's easy to lose focus and direction during the initial shock stage. Avoid behaviors that would be counterproductive and not help you work through this problem. Negative reactions also lessen the possibility of a marriage restoration.

Choose the Right Friends

Think carefully about the people with whom you spend time during this first shock stage. Don't keep away from people—you need support, encouragement, comfort and perspective—but think about who will give positive help.

Avoid people who would be unreal, telling you in essence, "Just tough it out; this happens to lots of people. Forget the past and move on." Other people to avoid are the superficially spiritual who say, "God loves you and has chosen this for you. Just think how special you're going to become because your husband has left you." Also avoid those people who take sides, such as Ann's mother did, attacking Bob when she learned he had abandoned Ann.

Be around people who are sincere and will not pretend that abandonment isn't a major disaster. Hang out with people who are practical in their help—who will visit frequently or take you out to dinner, a movie, a church event or community function. You need people who will keep you focused on the big picture of learning all you can about why this happened, the possibilities of the marriage being restored and the practical steps to be taken to recover from being thrown away.

These positive people can help strengthen your relationship to God as you participate together in Bible study or caring groups. Or they might send you little notes with special sections of Scripture that they have found to be personally strengthening. Sometimes a caring couple will stand with you, offering both a woman's and a man's point of view (and perhaps practical help as well: fixing the leaky faucet or helping you get the car repaired). Be sure to relate to them as a couple, not spending time alone with the man—both because you are vulnerable right now and to avoid any possibility of misunderstanding on anyone's part.

You need to be with people, but the people you choose will either help you recover from abandonment or drive you deeper into problems. Choose positive friends for this critical stage.

God—the Crucial Person

It pays to have close friends to talk to, but it's also a wonderful comfort to have a close personal relationship with God so that you can say, "God, help me, hear me, feel my pain!"

If the abandonment has been unexpected, as it was in Ann's case, your self-image may be smashed. Your life may have been centered primarily around your husband, children and home, and initially you will feel a massive attack on your selfhood.

In this critical moment you need to hear God, within the core of your being, speaking to you as he spoke to Joshua: "I will be with you just as I was with Moses; I will not abandon you or fail to help you" (Josh 1:5).

You need the same calming assurance as when God said to the nation of Israel, "Don't be afraid, for I have ransomed you; I have called you by name; you are mine. When you go through deep waters and great trouble, I will be with you. When you go through rivers of difficulty, you will not drown! When you walk through the fire of oppression, you will not be burned up—the flames will not consume you. For I am the Lord your God, your Savior" (Is 43:1-3).

The words of Scripture and the work of the Holy Spirit inside your mind will help you to keep focused on reality. And part of that reality is that you are a daughter of God. He loves and understands you and is with you in the middle of this mess.

The courage cards. Something that helped Ann during this first stage of shock was to write part of her daily Bible reading on a card. She selected a phrase, a promise or an insight that was encouraging to her. Then any time she felt stress during the day, she looked at her card and asked God to accomplish this in her life.

For example, Ann used the phrase from Joshua, "I will be with you just as I was with Moses; I will not abandon you or fail to help you." She carried this little card with her all during the day. Repeatedly she pulled it out and reminded herself that God was promising not to abandon her. Then she deliberately asked God not to leave her but to help her feel his promise and presence in her very soul.

Prayer therapy. Studies of medical treatment of the sick show that more positive results are obtained when prayer is included. In one study, half of the patients were given instructions, along with their medical treatment, to pray for God's presence, to receive God's forgiveness and to ask for physical healing. The other half was given medical treatment only, without the prayer therapy. The group that had medical treatment plus prayer therapy improved much faster than the other.[1]

Prayer not only puts you in touch with God; it helps you to focus in healing directions. As a result, the recovery time from psychological stress or physical illness is greatly reduced.

You may also have a friend who has a special gift of prayer. Ask that person to join you as you pray for the ability to cope and to be healed from the wounds caused by abandonment.

Picture God's presence. We encourage people in crisis to form the face of God in their mind and to see him giving peace and healing. Earlier we pointed out that filling our minds with a problem can make it seem worse than it really is and may set up a chain reaction of negative thoughts and events. Filling our minds with thoughts of God as our healer does exactly the opposite.

When you read a section from the Bible, such as Joshua 1:5, don't read it as only a statement about an era of history; hear it as God speaking directly to you. Visualize his face. Imagine him looking directly into your eyes, with his arms extended toward you and a kind look on his face as he speaks the words "I will not abandon you."

We encourage you to keep the mental picture of God helping you all the way through your recovery process. Picture God sitting across from you when you talk to a friend on the phone, when you think about your husband and the other woman, when you have to tell the children, when you are with friends or make that first difficult journey to church alone.

God is with you from the very moment you wake and through every small event all day long: from getting dressed to meeting with important clients at work to those last moments when you slip under the covers at night—alone. You're not really alone; God still promises that he will not abandon you. Set your mind on the peace he is giving to you as you go to sleep.

Think of your husband's abandonment as a package of pain. It's a box full of all sorts of things: your years of history together, the children and their special needs, your hopes for the future, the closeness that you had dreamed of with your husband, in addition to all the special problems you are facing. And don't forget—how could you?—the dreaded other woman.

All day long, as you are confronted with the issues related to your abandonment, mentally picture God with you. When you get ready to go to sleep, picture yourself handing the box to God. He takes the box, puts the lid on it, and says to you, "You've already worried about this too much; let me take care of this through the night as you sleep." Then picture God touching you as he says, "I love you, I won't abandon you, I'll be here in the night if you need me. Just go to sleep now."

During this time, when it may be very difficult to find someone with whom to talk, talk to God. When your mind wants to race off to ten thousand catastrophes, pick up your Bible, read it and let God give you hope.

For example, read Psalm 102, which gives you the opportunity to ventilate your distress and pain. Some of the phrases are "Listen to my plea! . . . My health is broken and my heart is sick. . . . My food is tasteless, and I have lost my appetite. I am reduced to skin and bones because of all my groaning and despair. . . . My enemies taunt me day after day and curse at me. I eat ashes instead of bread. My tears run down into my drink" (vv. 1, 3-5, 8-9). This psalm has a great prayer promise in it as well: "He will listen to the prayers of the destitute, for he is never too busy to heed their requests" (v. 17).

Then read Psalm 103, which overflows with God's love and care for us—his forgiveness, his healing and his tender mercy: "He is like a father to us, tender and sympathetic to those who reverence him. For he knows we are but dust, and that our days are few and brief, like grass, like flowers, blown by the wind and gone forever. But the lovingkindness of the Lord is from everlasting to everlasting, to those who reverence him" (vv. 13-17).

Sometimes you don't need to read large sections of Scripture to sense God's deep caring for you. God touched me (Jim) from Psalm 97:10-11 recently as I was working on this book: "The Lord loves those who hate evil; he protects the lives of his people, and rescues them from the wicked. Light is sown for the godly and joy for the good." As I came to those verses, I focused on

the five things that seemed to leap off the page at me:
- ☐ The Lord loves
- ☐ The Lord protects
- ☐ The Lord rescues
- ☐ The Lord gives light
- ☐ The Lord gives joy

It was a wonderful reminder to me that when my life seems difficult, God is there. His love is constant; he is always present, protecting and rescuing. In the black nights of life, he throws light on us and gives joy. Our situation hasn't changed, but we receive joy and peace because we know that God is in charge.

A Personal Note

Sally and I have been through some heavy-duty stuff. I grew up in a dysfunctional home and didn't realize for many years that the reason I had few childhood memories was that I was blocking out pain of the past. When I did begin to remember, dealing with the rubbish was an agonizing experience.

Our lives have also been tested by many hard times in our immediate family. One of our daughters was dyslexic and did not learn to read until she was an adult. Another of our daughters had heart problems, and a third had her leg amputated because of bone cancer when she was sixteen years old.

In addition, we've experienced some rocky times in our marriage. During my mid-life crisis I was ready to abandon Sally. I wanted to leave her and the girls and the church I was pastoring far behind me and just drive south forever.

We've also faced severe financial stress. On one occasion we were down to only a can of pickled beets in the cupboard (who could ever stand those?). Another time we had to personally assume $100,000 in debts because of our radio ministry.

In recent years we have been struggling with Sally's breast cancer. She had a tumor larger then a walnut removed, and the cancer had spread to sixteen lymph nodes. The chemotherapy to cure the cancer has left several debilitating side effects.

So, when we say that knowing God as a personal friend and visualizing his presence and care can be helpful, we are speaking from personal experience.

We urge you to continually picture yourself moving toward the wisdom recorded in Psalm 112, which says that the person who trusts God "does not fear bad news, nor live in dread of what may happen. For she is settled in her mind that Jehovah will take care of her" (v. 7, adapted).

As you become more convinced that God will take care of you, even though bad news items continue to jolt you, you will have a deep, quiet settledness because you are trusting that God *will* take care of you.

One other tip as you finish this chapter: a divorced woman who read an early draft of this book said we should encourage you to read this chapter over and over again as you recover. She said it would help you to keep stabilized.

Whom have I in heaven but you? And I desire no one on earth as much as you! My health fails; my spirits droop, yet God remains! He is the strength of my heart; he is mine forever! (Ps 73:25-26)

— 8 —

Restore
the Relationship
If Possible

W*E'VE HAD THE PRIVILEGE OF SWIMMING AND SNORKELING IN* some great places around the world. It's fun being in the ocean. The salt water gives buoyancy so staying afloat takes less effort, and it's great snorkeling around reefs to get a close-up view of the fascinating way God has "painted" tropical fish.

Sometimes I (Jim) like to swim with several bread crusts tucked into my bathing suit. When I get to a spot with lots of fish, I pull out the bread and break it into little pieces. Soon I find myself in the midst of a fish swarm as hundreds of them crowd in for a little snack of bread.

Then comes the part I don't like—getting out of the water and taking one of those cold showers at the beach. It's necessary to wash off the sticky salt water—if you don't, your skin starts to itch and you feel miserable.

I hate cold showers! Each time I come out of the water, I'm

faced with a dilemma: shall I try to get by without it (and endure the itching) or shall I suffer the agony of the cold shower in order to feel more comfortable afterward?

Salvage operations. Trying to save a breaking marriage is far more difficult and painful than taking the cold beach shower. In stage one, the woman is angry, shocked and numb. She feels betrayed and abandoned, not only by her husband but sometimes by other family members and friends as well. To even think about saving the relationship is almost impossible—what she may really want to do is kill him.

It may seem that we are asking you to do the impossible, think the impossible. You've been hurt, run over by a truck, betrayed, misunderstood, exploited. *Why should I even try?* you say. *He's the one that walked out!* Your pain is terribly, terribly real. But if you skip over this stage in the healing process, you will never successfully negotiate the next stages and will never fully recover from abandonment.

You believe in marriage; you have believed in *your* marriage. You aren't in favor of divorce. Even if the chances look slim, the right thing to do may be to try, with your best efforts, to get communication flowing so that you and your husband can consider whether reconciliation is possible.

It is important for your own personal growth, as well, that you try to restore your marriage. If you don't try, you'll be like a person who is afraid to drive again after a terrible auto accident—never again able to have the benefit of using a car. For your own future health—as painful as it will be—*you must try!*

If only. A common thread of anxiety runs through people who are divorced and then remarried. Three or four years into the next marriage, when everything is not as wonderful as was hoped, the partners begin to ask themselves, *Could I have saved my first marriage if I had worked harder?* and *How much did I contribute to the breakup of my marriage?*

The people who ask these questions after remarriage are generally those who have skipped over stage two. They did not work at trying to salvage the first relationship. If people put out massive effort to grow, change and restore their marriage, and it still does not come back together, then they have a sense of freedom as they give up. They think, *Now it is right to walk away. I did the very best I could, and I never have to feel guilty before myself, God or other people.*

So it is *very* crucial that you not skip over this second stage of trying to restore the marriage. It may be the last thing you want to do—like that cold shower on the beach. But if you omit this stage, your unresolved issues may result in more personal struggles—and more marriage problems if you should choose to remarry.

Usually people are not ready to enter stage two until some of the anger and shock of stage one have passed. You can tell you're entering the second stage when you begin to ask yourself questions such as *I wonder what some of the forces were that made it easy for him to abandon our marriage.* When you come to see that the other woman is simply a symptom of a greater problem and not the problem itself, when you wonder what the vacuums were in your husband's life that influenced him to make this drastic move, you are entering stage two.

Pressure from others. Some of your family members or friends will not understand the change in your direction. The last they heard, you were expressing anger at your husband for abandoning you. Now your perception is changing and you've decided to try to rebuild your relationship. Some people won't be able to fathom that. They'll try to push you ahead into stage three, accepting the abandonment. They'll urge you to "just forget him and get on with your life." You must resist their strong push and sincerely work at trying to repair the relationship so that you can be emotionally healthy in the future.

It's important to realize that you face a risk of more emotional damage as you try to rebuild the marriage relationship. You are likely to receive more rejection from your husband, at first, if he doesn't want reconciliation or is afraid you're going to make demands on him. And that rejection may force you back into stage one—feeling again the abandonment and anger that were so intense at first.

Remember not to be manipulated by well-meaning friends or by your husband's anger. Keep focused on your tasks for stage two.

Take responsibility only for yourself. Don't accept blame for your husband's part in the marriage failure. Focus on controlling and stabilizing yourself. You can't control your husband, but you can control yourself. Blaming your husband, focusing on the past and beating up on yourself will be counterproductive.

As Ann moved past the initial shock stage, she began to get some new insights. One day she told us, "It may sound crazy, but I can understand why Jennifer would want Bob. Her reasons are the same reasons I want him. He's a great guy, and maybe that's why it hurts so terribly that he's left me."

Later she asked us, "Do you think I've done something that made it easy for Bob to leave our marriage?" She told us that she had been wrestling with this question and her feelings about the situation were changing. She wondered if she had unknowingly contributed to the breakup.

It was Bob who had walked out, and we told Ann again that she did *not* need to bear guilt about that. But we felt Ann was ready to face the next stage, so we put the question directly to her: "How hard are you willing to work to try to restore this relationship?"

Ann asked, "What do you mean?"

We responded, "The illness in your marriage is not like a two-week bout with flu. If you want to attempt to put this back together, you need to commit yourself for many months to work on your own personal growth and on understanding Bob and his reasons for abandonment.

"We're not talking only about a long period of time; we also mean working intensely, being willing to accept additional disappointment from Bob and being willing to face any of your own marital inadequacies that may have contributed to this breakup. Give it some time. Think about it and talk to God about your decision. When we talk again, maybe you'll have a clearer direction.

"But remember, if you skip over this salvage stage and don't really make a sincere attempt at reconstructing your relationship, you are likely to regret your decision somewhere down the road. You may always wonder whether you should have put more energy into rebuilding this marriage."

How to Revive the Relationship

A few days later Ann called us and said that she had decided to try to save her marriage. She didn't feel hopeful, but she did want her husband back. She wanted to do her part. Bob had a major responsibility in all this, too, but she was not in control of his desires or actions. Over the next several weeks we helped Ann explore a number of areas in the salvaging process. We hope that as you understand Ann's growth, you too will have the will to grow and change.

1. Understand why he abandoned you. It was crucial for Ann to understand the extreme pressures on Bob that had influenced him as he made this drastic change in their marriage and put everyone at such high risk. Ann already realized that Jennifer was not the problem. That discovery helped Ann look beyond Jennifer into Bob's experience to understand him and what he was going through.

Ann made a list of some of the factors that could have affected his decision. This was an ongoing project for her. Over several weeks she began to see a pattern. She listed such things as:

☐ Bob's dissatisfaction with his lack of advancement at work

☐ His feeling that he was not as successful as other men in his college class

☐ His disappointment that he didn't have a closer relationship with his children

☐ His sadness that he had never connected with his father as a mentor or friend

☐ His panic that life was passing too quickly after his fortieth birthday

☐ His worry that he was losing his physical attractiveness

As the weeks went along, Ann added other items such as:

☐ I was too preoccupied with my job to listen to his career problems

☐ I was too busy helping the kids get everywhere they needed to go—the kids sort of became more important to me than Bob

☐ I used to flirt with him a lot when we were first married, but then I just became too busy

☐ I teased him about losing his hair and getting an inner-tube tummy

Ann realized her list was the description of a man who felt life was cheating him. Finally he had made a desperate attempt to recapture some of what he felt he was losing. Jennifer simply became the available person who would help him in his quest to feel good about himself.

2. Be prepared for hard work. Ann started reading books on marriage and divorce, mid-life problems, forgiveness and so on. (Some of those we've listed in the notes may be helpful to you at this point.[1]) Ann reminded herself that this wasn't going to be an easy task, nor would it be over quickly. She was not a superwoman; she was like every other woman who has been discarded. Some days she had great drive, ambition and vision to save her marriage. Other times she didn't care at all. At those times she said she'd be glad if she never saw Bob again, and she would shout at us, "I'm not the one who walked out on the marriage—*he* did!" And she was right.

After she had exploded, she would usually sit quietly for a few moments and then begin to ask the important questions such as "But why did he walk out on our marriage?" Her first reaction was to say it was all Bob's fault. But the more she understood Bob's "whys" for leaving and what part she had played in his reasons for leaving, the more willing she was to work hard on the relationship.

3. Reduce the pressure. As Ann saw additional reasons why Bob had left the marriage, she began to realize that both of them had been under a great deal of pressure. Bob felt unfulfilled at work and unable to communicate with his children. Ann seemed to be distracted by her job and the kids and uninterested in him romantically. He seemed to feel his only role with the family was to pay the bills and keep everything repaired and running smoothly.

As Ann gained more insight during their separation, she looked for ways to reduce the pressure on Bob whenever he had contact with the family. She coached the children to tell their dad how much he had always meant to them and what a good dad he was for them. She also arranged for appliance repair and yard work to be done by other people so the house and yard were not needing Bob's attention when he stopped by to see the kids. (Some women won't have the luxury of hiring help, but perhaps they can call on friends to help for a short duration.)

In some sense Ann was in competition with Jennifer. Jennifer was not asking Bob to repair her washing machine, pay her bills, get new tires on her car. Their relationship was focused more on having fun. As Ann realized that, she planned that anytime Bob was around the family, they would have a positive and upbeat time, not one of pressure, accusations and chores.

Yes, sometime later she would need to confront him regarding his bad choices about the affair. But her first focus was on trying to rebuild the relationship. It helped to imagine how she would have handled it if Bob had broken his leg playing football with some college guys. She would have been upset at his foolish choice—but she would also have done all she could to help him recover.

4. Meet his needs. Ann told us about her insights and discoveries about Bob in the early months of their dating. One thing that stuck in Ann's memory was when he told her that he had little or no relationship with his family. At first it was hard for Ann to believe, because Bob seemed to be in such control of his life. But as he shared, she began to understand how deeply disconnected from his father he felt and how much he needed to be affirmed.

"From that point on," Ann said, "I did everything I could to build him up. I tried to encourage him that he was a worthwhile person regardless of whether he felt connected to family or not."

Each time she had learned a new insight about Bob, she had tried to help him know that she accepted and loved him. As Ann reflected on how much she had reached out to Bob in their early years, she made a startling statement: "You know, after we turned thirty, I just didn't do that anymore. Maybe I stopped listening to Bob; maybe we were too busy. Whatever it was, I began to be more distant. I see now that I stopped meeting his real needs."

We told Ann that people are attracted to each other because they meet each other's needs. And they stay together because they continue to meet each other's needs. If there was any hope for their marriage to be restored, it would be necessary to focus on understanding Bob at *this* age and meeting his current needs. (Understand that if we had been counseling Bob at this point, we would have urged him to do the same toward Ann.)

5. *Apologize.* In one session, Ann tried as much as she could to put herself into Bob's mind and to look out at the world through Bob's eyes. She asked aloud, "From Bob's point of view, who is at fault in this marriage? From Bob's point of view, am I a good wife? From Bob's point of view, what are the events or who are the people causing stress in his life?"

Ann sat quietly for several minutes, trying as honestly as possible to view the world through his eyes. Finally, she said slowly, "He sees the world very differently than I do. If I limit myself to think through his mind, I can even understand why he would be attracted to Jennifer."

Ann then specifically identified—from Bob's point of view— the areas where she had "failed" as a wife. Because Ann had been wrestling with some of these ideas for several weeks, she cautiously listed off that she:

☐ had become too busy

☐ hadn't sensed his growing stress at work

☐ hadn't realized how much his disconnection from the children bothered him

☐ had not given him the personal affirmation that he needed

☐ had not understood how turning forty affected him

☐ had not continued the girlfriend role of flirting and being romantic with him

After Ann had finished listing the areas where she might have "failed" as a wife, we asked her, "How would Bob react if you apologized to him for these failures?"

"I think he'd be shocked. I don't think I've told Bob that I was sorry about any major thing in our lives for years."

Ann decided to invite Bob out for coffee, basically for the purpose of apologizing. She wanted to talk to him specifically about these concerns:

☐ assure him that she was not trying to manipulate him to return to the marriage

□ directly apologize and take responsibility for her areas of failure as she saw them

□ reassure him that she still loved him

□ express to him that even though this separation and the affair had been very hard, it had caused an overall positive growth in her life

Even though she would apologize very directly to Bob, she would not expect some kind of magical turnaround. Men tend to process emotional information slowly. Even if Bob appreciated her apology, he would not likely tell her so, because he would fear that he would be committing himself to reenter the marriage. He probably would not say, "I'm sorry I've been such a jerk; please forgive me." He was not at that decision point yet.

Ann did meet with Bob, and she did apologize. She noticed a very relieved look on his face, even though his only response was, "Well, thank you for saying that."

6. *Be a friend.* Ann was doing very difficult things. She was the one trying to save the marriage. Bob was very passive. But we encouraged her to keep focusing on trying to make her marriage work, with a deeper level of understanding and commitment. If the marriage was not saved, she would still have more peace because she had tried. It was crucial for her own psychological and spiritual recovery to know that she had done her very best to make the marriage work if, at some point in the future, she began to question whether she had done enough.

Basically, Bob had only one friend, Jennifer. He had caused a disruption in almost every other relationship in his life. He had caused an uneasiness at work because of the office romance. Because of his guilty feelings, he had dropped his friends at church and no longer attended the Thursday evening dinner group. He had brought about an alienation between himself and his relatives on both sides of the family. His children were angry at him. So the only friends Bob had, besides Jennifer, were a group of frustrated, recently divorced men who got together often and consoled themselves with how good the single life was.

The sudden change in Bob's friendship status was taking its toll. Temporarily, he thought he could be a hermit and isolate himself in his cozy apartment with Jennifer. But before long, Bob needed a broader group of friends. And he wanted to reconnect with his children and with the family history he had lost when he left.

Ann potentially could play a strategic role by being Bob's very best friend. Jennifer was the newcomer; Ann had a lifetime of experiences with Bob. If Ann could reduce the pressure and take a friendship approach to Bob, a time would probably come when he would quite easily drop into a conversation with her, which might be the beginning of a renewed friendship.

7. *Listen.* Before the breakup, both Bob and Ann had become so busy in their own worlds of activity that they were not connecting or listening to each other. But now, whenever they had any contact by phone or when he came to see the kids, Ann was listening for any word or phrase that might suggest pain in Bob's life in the following areas:

□ dissatisfaction at work, fear of being fired or disqualified from future promotion

□ general confusion about life itself

□ wishing he could be young again

□ unhappiness because of the loss of friends

□ missing the children

□ reflections on the good times he and Ann had had together

"Listen to Bob's phrases," we told Ann. "Unconsciously or deliberately, he may be dropping a few words or phrases to see how you handle them. You could follow up with, 'I am sorry you're wrestling with stuff at work; I know this is a hard time. I pray for you all the time.' These kinds of remarks indicate you actually are listening and want to be a friend. They will help Bob reconnect to you.

"On the other hand, when he hints at some of his struggles and you respond with, 'Well, it serves you right. Look what you've done to me!' then you drive the wedge deeper between the two of you."

8. *Build his self-esteem.* Bob's self-esteem was currently being bolstered from two directions. His divorced male friends were cheering him on and Jennifer was assuring him that he was doing the right thing. Most of his former friends were very critical of Bob and his abandonment of Ann. If Ann could begin to encourage Bob's self-esteem, Bob might gain the strength he needed to work on the issues he was facing, and, ultimately, their marriage might have a chance.

When people are under a great deal of stress, they tend to look for people or experiences that will give them peace and relief—and they avoid potentially painful situations. Bob's affair with Jennifer was a way of trying to escape his pressures. Jennifer was the one who was stabilizing his self-image and giving him the strength to face life. If Ann could do the same, then Bob would not need Jennifer.

Ann could affirm Bob anytime he dropped one of those little phrases indicating that he felt uncomfortable about his age, was confused about life, missed the kids or was struggling with work.

Small things count. When Ann saw him, she commented, "You're looking good—but then, you always did." When he dropped off some presents for the kids, Ann affirmed Bob for caring and for wrapping them himself. She was certainly not going to compliment him for his abandonment, for the affair with Jennifer or for the pain he had caused her! But she could affirm him by telling him that she valued some of his traits. "Bob, I've always appreciated the fact that you are sensitive to people's needs. Even though you're struggling with a lot of issues right now, I believe God is going to lead you through this whole process. You're going to end up being a better man." A small approval given each time she talked with him would perhaps help him realize he didn't have to go the Jennifer route to get affirmation.

9. *Change and grow.* Before a man finally decides to leave and marry another woman, he's going to look again at his marriage to decide if it's actually as bad as he thought or if there is some possibility of making it work. It is crucial for you to do all you can from your side to give the marriage a chance.

You will never be able to reestablish your former marriage. In a sense, *that* marriage is dead. Any future relationship with your husband must be a revised one, with new rules and new commitments. Your mate needs to see that you are working at it—you're changing and open to new rules.

In addition, your personal growth will bring something fresh into the relationship. If you've always wanted to paint, then why not take an art class at the community college? Follow your heart and do some of the things you've been putting off while you've been raising children.

Perhaps some of your new growth areas can connect with your husband's interests. For example, if he is on a physical fitness kick and if you've been wanting to work on your weight, this would be a good time to get your body in shape. Accomplishing your goal will feel good to you and will connect with his fitness interest. Taking a class or developing a skill such as sculpting, sewing, even flying a plane will make you a more interesting person to be around. Or it may be time to enroll in a program of further education. Whatever you choose should be for you first, though, not just to win back your husband.

You must put your heart fully into the process of trying to renew the relationship. Otherwise, later on, whether you remarry or not, you're going to ask yourself hundreds of times, *What if I'd worked harder? Could I have pulled that relationship back together again? Could I have been more flexible? What if I had said I was sorry and tried to be his friend? Could I have made a difference?* Yes, it takes two to heal a marriage. You can't control his responses; maybe all of this effort will accomplish nothing in terms of the marriage. But it will accomplish something good in you as you are able to say, "I did my best."

Words of Caution

Perhaps you can identify with much of Ann's experience. It's important that you remind yourself that this is new territory for you. Remember that the abandonment situation is volatile. You and your husband are both very vulnerable. With that in mind, let's look at some of the "don'ts."

1. Don't take your husband back until both of you have gone through an extensive healing and counseling process. Sometimes, in the midst of the wife's being honest and understanding, the husband feels he has really blown it and is swept away with her kindness. He says, "I'm really, really sorry." Then they hug and kiss and think everything will be okay. A number of couples have reported that the relationship changed so much in just a few moments that it was electrifying. In fact, in the heat of passion they made love and both of them found it a mind-blowing, exhilarating experience.

Don't be fooled. There are still long-term reasons why the relationship fell apart. Unless those reasons are corrected, your husband will be attracted to any one of a thousand other women who are able and wanting to meet his needs.

Don't take him back too early. You can tell him that this meeting was really great, you love him and you're grateful for who he is. You can give him genuine affirmation. You may even want to spend time playing together, but don't let him move home yet. Tell him you want to make sure that you both don't blow it again. Ask him, "Would you be willing to go with me to counseling so that we can make sure it will last?"

2. *Don't become a victim—of a relative, of other men or of your children.* Don't allow relatives to take out their anger against your husband on you. Sometimes a jealous relative has envied your marriage or your husband's success and now will use this opportunity to victimize and punish you. Avoid those people.

Remember that you are vulnerable to anyone who will listen and understand you. Many men would like to care for you, "understand you"—and get you into bed. They want to help you with your "needs." Yes, you have physical, sexual and companionship needs, and some men would like to exploit your vulnerability. If you need to talk to someone about your physical needs, talk to a close woman friend.

Don't let your children victimize you. A temptation when a marriage is falling apart is for each parent to attempt to win the affection and support of their children by giving them anything they want. Kids quickly spot parental vulnerability and know how to exploit it for their own benefit. It's easy for your life with the children to become nonstop Disneyland. But you need to let your kids know that the same boundaries apply now as when their dad was at home.

3. *Don't ignore your boundaries.* During this transitional time you may feel very needy and be vulnerable to exploitation. Fully understand the edges of your emotional boundaries. Be willing to say to someone, "Please, don't do that." You must not allow people to cross your boundaries because you feel needy or because you are too embarrassed to tell them to stop. If you don't have the emotional courage to tell people to stop, then get away from them and stay away until the issue is fully resolved.

4. *Don't accept unjustified reasons for your husband's abandonment.* Don't believe anyone who says it's all your fault. It's

true you may bear some of the blame—but your husband also is at fault. It may have been that he didn't have the courage to tell you that he needed more from you, or that he never recovered from childhood damage, or that he has some sort of addiction.

Sometimes when a husband is about ready to come back, he views his wife's willingness to apologize, change and be conciliatory as a sign of weakness. A husband may then use this opportunity to exploit his wife and manipulate her with unreasonable demands.

Even though at this stage in your recovery you are not focusing on his failure, you must remember that you are not the only one who failed in this marriage relationship. And you are not the one who ran away from it. Ultimately, your husband has to work through the issues, acknowledge his part and make the appropriate changes, or a good marriage will never be possible. Both of you are going to need professional counseling and much prayer.

5. Don't blast your husband. Through the early stages of your recovery, your temptation may be not only to confront him angrily but also to hurt and punish him. Emotionally charged confrontations that contain anger, spite, sarcasm or a raised voice create a very hostile environment. Generally, the other person will run away to protect himself or will retaliate.

Since the focus is on trying to restore the relationship at this stage, the general rule of thumb is not to confront so early in the separation. Save confrontations for later stages. Even then, we urge you to keep those confrontations on a very factual, nonemotional level.

The Power of Prayer

During stage two, as you try to rebuild the relationship, you will find yourself going above and beyond the call of duty many times. You will do all the positive things, trying to help your husband work through his problems—but you will probably get no emotional nourishment from him at all. Therefore, it is very, very important that you keep a strong connection to God and that you vigorously draw on the power of prayer.

In the back of your Bible you may find a section called a concordance. Look up the word *prayer.* You will find dozens of references to prayer. Look up each verse in the four Gospels (the first four books of the New Testament). If the verse contains a promise about prayer, write it on a card and refer to it often. This is a promise that God is making to *you.*

Most of the promises in the first four books of the New Testament are promises that Jesus himself made to his believers. Take these promises at face value and specifically express your needs to God in prayer. Visualize God working deep within your emotions to help you become the person you want to be.

Picture God also working deep within your mate's heart, helping him to grow and change as he works through the issues he is facing. Also picture God working in each of your children, protecting them and helping them to become whole persons— persons who will be stronger teenagers and adults because of what God is doing in them now.

As with Ann, we suggest you draw on God's promises and trust him to work. We also recommend that you find two or three women who will be close confidantes and will offer prayer support. Agree together to pray specifically for God to work in the life of each person involved in this abandonment. Pray even if you are angry at your mate, at the "other woman" or at God.

Remember not to pray generically. Don't simply say, "God bless my husband and the kids and me, amen." Rather, pray that God will help each family member let go of the anger and bitterness, turning it over to him. Ask God to reduce the dependency that your husband and the other woman have on each other. Pray for God to arrange specific opportunities for you to speak to your children and husband in ways to affirm and strengthen each one them. Ask him for wisdom and insight in each situation.

Remember, God has given you an opportunity to talk to him personally and to enlist his aid in this problem. Through prayer, you can touch the very core of your husband's being, even though you may not be able to see him often or connect with him very deeply when you do meet. Prayer will help you stay focused on trying to restore your marriage.

Show me the path where I should go, O Lord; point out the right road for me to walk. Lead me; teach me; for you are the God who gives me salvation. I have no hope except in you. (Ps 25:4-5)

— 9 —

From Pain
to Acceptance

*D*URING OUR COUNSELING TIME WITH ANN, SHE KEPT ASKING, "HOW much longer do I have to go through this? Six months, a year, two years? Where am I in this whole process of healing? Am I just getting started or am I almost finished?"

About six months after Bob abandoned Ann, a very distinct change came in their relationship that signaled a new stage in Ann's recovery. Bob filed for divorce. Ann and Bob lived in a state with a no-fault divorce law, which meant that in thirty days their marriage would be over. Then, two weeks before the divorce was final, Bob told her that he was going to marry Jennifer the day after the divorce was finalized.

The world crashed for Ann. She had worked so hard to rebuild the relationship. She was growing and changing in many ways and had become a more interesting and desirable person—yet Bob ignored all of Ann's growth. He wanted to start over with someone else. He didn't care about the cost. And he didn't care who got hurt in the process—his abandonment of Ann was final.

When Ann walked into our office, she dropped into the chair and disintegrated into a jumbled mass of anger, fear, self-pity and despair. Her personality seemed very much like the wad of Kleenex lying on her lap.

We were deeply concerned for Ann, because she talked of the uselessness of going on. "Why did I give all those years to Bob and our marriage, only to have it smashed now? No, it's worse than smashed—this is even worse than death! If he had died, everyone would gather around me. I could remember all the good things about him, and there would be an honorable ending to our relationship.

"But what do I have now? My husband has rejected me! By his actions he says I'm not worthy to be his wife. He doesn't even care about the kids. We're all just dirt to be scraped off the bottom of his shoe as he walks away into a new life."

Ann was no longer at stage two in her recovery, trying to save the marriage. She had regressed into stage one—the shock stage. Really, she was bouncing back and forth. Part of her wanted to move on. She had done her best to restore the relationship, but Bob would not give Ann any hope at all for reconciliation.

As you move gradually toward stage three, acceptance, keep focused on what feelings and tasks will help you:

☐ *Feelings:* Affirm yourself for doing your best. Trust God to work to heal the past and give you a future of hope.

☐ *Tasks:* Release your past marriage and your former husband to God. Redirect your thoughts away from past pain to your future.

But Ann was not fully ready to move toward acceptance. She needed more time for her feelings to be at stage one, shock. She needed to feel the horrible process again. After Ann poured out her heart for about forty minutes, I (Jim) shared with her some information from a book titled *On Death and Dying*.

The author, Elisabeth Kübler-Ross, outlines five distinct emotional stages through which a person goes as he or she handles the grief that accompanies death. Ann had correctly identified the situation. This was a death—their marriage had died. It was actually worse than death.

Within stage three of her recovery, Ann would be going through many of the emotional stages experienced by a person who has lost a friend or mate in death or who faces his or her own death

The five stages listed by Kübler-Ross are

Denial—"It's not me—it's not true!"

Anger—"Why me?"

Bargaining—"Can't we postpone this?"

Depression—"All is lost."

Acceptance—"I'm ready for my new life."[1]

1. Denial. In the first period of grieving her loss, Ann experienced a great deal of denial: "This really isn't happening to me." This is a normal response. However, if you grieve your loss in a healthy way, you won't end up with the problem of denial on top of abandonment and then feel guilty about denying.

Denial is common, but it didn't change the reality that Bob had abandoned Ann. There was no way to turn the clock back to the early days of marriage. When a person dies, you cannot bring him or her back to life by denying that death has taken place. In the same way, marriage cannot be brought back to life by denying that it has died.

It's okay for you to express your feelings of denial, but in the back of your mind, you must remember that denial is not going to change the situation. Ultimately you must, and you will, move on to other, healthier stages.

2. Anger. Anger is another part of grieving. Ann replayed some of the anger she had expressed in the shock stage. She had been angry at Bob's first announcement that he was leaving and planned to marry Jennifer. But she was also angry now, because she had worked hard all these months, trying her very best to bring the marriage back together—and it didn't happen.

Ann was extremely angry at Bob and Jennifer. She surprised herself that she was also angry at other people—relatives and church friends. She lashed out at the women in her small peer support group and at us as counselors, because we were the ones who had encouraged her to work hard to restore her marriage.

But what shocked Ann the most was her extreme anger at God. "Why didn't God change the situation? Why did he let our marriage deteriorate?" She even asked, "Why did God allow us to get married in the first place? At the time it seemed so clearly God's will, and now it seems so terribly, terribly wrong."

It's all right for you to be angry. Short-term anger is productive because it helps you identify with yourself and the intensity of your feelings. But you must not get stuck at the anger stage; you must move through this pain and finally come to acceptance.

3. *Bargaining and replay.* Some people *bargain* with God: "If you bring our marriage back together, I'll change." But for most people, it's not so much bargaining as replaying the failed times—regrets for the thoughtlessness and unnecessary pain.

Replay is a sort of fantasy time when you think back to all the good things that you did together, plus all that you wish you had done in your marriage—the experiences you never got around to. You'll remember the times you blew it and wish you had a chance to change it. Replay time is the desire to go back and relive life, to make all the magical changes so you wouldn't end up in this abandoned state.

Thousands of events will replay in your mind. Replaying is profitable because it helps you focus on how to live differently in the future. However, replaying the events of your marriage will never bring your marriage back. Ultimately, for your healing you must move beyond this position.

All three of these periods mentioned by Kübler-Ross, and commonly accepted by other experts, can be experienced at the same time or one after another in sequence. More likely, you will bounce back and forth among the stages. From our point of view, it's probably better to look at these three periods as a stage of *reaction*. You react with denial, you react with anger, you react by bargaining and replaying. These are the feelings people have in the beginning of recovery.

Don't beat up on yourself. Don't feel you have to respond according to someone else's agenda or stages. These levels are simply guidelines to let you know where you are in this process. Most of all, don't feel guilty if you find yourself skipping back and forth, going back again and again to one of the old feelings, such as anger.

4. *Depression/withdrawal.* The fourth stage is distinctly different from the first three. It is depression, accompanied by withdrawal into yourself, temporarily cutting off friends. Both of these words express a sense of hopelessness.

You experience hopelessness, in the first place, because of the abandonment. Then you feel hopeless because you worked so hard to restore the marriage and it didn't happen. Finally, you have a sense of sadness as you look back over your marriage and realize that many things happened that you didn't realize were leading to abandonment. Withdrawal can include despondency: *Things are so hopeless I might as well drop out of life.*

You may find yourself wanting to give up on everything—your small group, the church, your counseling sessions, even God himself. In fact, you may lose confidence in your ability to do anything right, especially in relationships.

At times you will emotionally go around the rooms of your heart, drawing all the drapes and turning off the lights. Don't be afraid of those times. Depression and withdrawal can actually be quiet times when God brings about healing in you.

5. *Acceptance.* As we see it, a gap shows up in the list of grief periods—a gap between depression/withdrawal and the final level, which is acceptance. We keep asking, "What is going on in the time after depression/withdrawal and before the final acceptance? What's happening inside the person? Why is she finally able to move to acceptance?"

We believe the gap is a special place where God is working. In an almost indescribable healing, God brings about the ability to accept the abandonment and move on. It's as if you and God are alone in Elijah's cave. Elijah was an Old Testament prophet who was in deep depression, hiding in a cave and fearing for his life. God met him in the cave and in a quiet voice calmed his fears and gave him hope for the future. (See 1 Kings 17:1—19:17, especially 19:8-17.) God is caring for you and speaking imperceptibly to you in his quiet voice, giving healing to your soul and hope for your future.

As you move on from the pain of your husband's abandonment, you will need to come to final acceptance. Until you do, you cannot start the reconstruction of your life. Acceptance comes about very gradually. It's not so much by an act of your will as by a quiet surge from within you. You won't be fully aware that it is happening—until it has happened.

Acceptance can be compared to a wave in the ocean as it makes its move toward shore. When you look at the ocean, it's almost impossible to pick out an individual wave. But as it moves closer to the shore, it takes shape and rises higher and higher. The wave finally curls over and the whitecap begins to form. Then the foam shows underneath the curl—and finally the huge wall of water crashes against the shore.

As the wave breaks, you sense its power and majesty; yet you may wonder, *Where was the wave all the time when it was only a part of the ocean?* So it will be with you as you start to accept the reality of your husband's abandonment. At first, you won't feel the change, but increasingly you will discern a sense of power, movement and completion.

In fact, as you come fully to the acceptance stage, you'll look back and wonder, *Why was I such a pessimist? Why didn't I get through those earlier stages more quickly?*

It's as if in the earlier stages you said, *Oh, this is terrible, half of the pie is gone.* Now your view changes as you say, *Wow, this is great, half of the pie is left!* You'll begin to see yourself not as a poor, unfortunate divorced person—a victim of abandonment—but as a whole person who is becoming stronger than ever before. You are more experienced now, and you more fully understand life, marriage and other people's struggles.

As you move on in your healing process, believe it or not, you'll look back on this abandonment as bringing about some very positive growth in your life. You will never forget the pain of this experience, but your hurt will be softened as God enables you to see, enjoy and use the qualities in your more mature personality. You'll finally be able to say, "My marriage wasn't healed—but I was."

How to Move from Pain to Acceptance

Some important steps will help the abandoned woman move past the terrible pain to an acceptance that enables her to move on with the rest of her life.

Press toward realism. Try not to get stuck on such thoughts as "what should be," "I deserve" or "you owe me." These feelings are okay to express, but keep coming back to *what is.* Most of the earlier stages focus on pain, shock and anger. Many of these feelings are punitive. You want to get even, want your rights, keep demanding that things be different. All of that focus is on fantasy, not on *what is.* Focusing on *what is* will move you more quickly to acceptance than focusing on the dream of what *could be* or *should be*.

Keep connected to help. The temptation is to either storm around in anger and frustration or be depressed and withdrawn. In both of these modes, people do not tend to look for help. Keep bringing yourself back to the reality that you need help.

Let people help you. The Bible teaches us that each Christian should be using his or her gifts and abilities to help other Christians. Stay connected to your prayer group, even though many times you may wonder whether prayer works. Keep connected to God even if you are very angry at him. It's okay to rant and rave at God. He can take it. And even in the midst of your angry outbursts, be assured that he still loves you.

Keep connected to professional counseling help. A good counselor will give you a safe environment to ventilate. He or she will also become the prod, or stimulus, to move you along in the healing process. In short, don't hide, even when that is what you would like to do. Stay connected to people and to help.

Choose a time to confront. In the earlier stages we encouraged the abandoned woman not to confront yet. Now it's time to take that risk. Confrontation tends to force people to make a decision. It's worth the risk of confronting now—you have nothing to lose. Confrontation too early in a marital breakup will tend to drive the running partner farther away, but that's not the issue now.

Since Bob had filed for divorce and announced that he was going to marry Jennifer the day after the divorce, Ann had nothing to lose by very direct confrontation. We encouraged her to speak specifically to Bob about what he was giving up, how she still loved him and how very, very angry she was at him and at Jennifer. Bob needed to hear the double truth that (1) neither she nor he had done everything right in their marriage but (2) that didn't give him permission to have an affair and kill their marriage.

Sometimes the shock of confrontation will cause the running husband to stop in his tracks and rethink his abandonment. We have found, though, that more than ninety percent of the time confrontation tends to alienate the husband and commit him more fully in the direction of running away.

However, confrontation has a very positive effect on the abandoned partner. She is speaking up, telling her whole heart and expressing her pain to the very person who is causing the pain. Confrontation is painful for her, but in the process her self-image is vastly strengthened. Confrontation helps her to sense that she is in charge. And it very subtly moves her along the path toward acceptance as she dumps the pain onto true person who has caused most of it.

Grieve the loss. Grieving is not living in the past, wishing it could be different. Grieving is feeling that this is awful. *I have lost my marriage. I have been abandoned, and it feels indescribably horrible.* The grief is not only for what has been lost from the past, but also for what will never be experienced in the future.

Grieving the loss helps you to face and accept the reality that you have been abandoned. Grieving also helps you ventilate the pain and frees you so that you are able to move into acceptance. You may be tempted to skip the grieving step because of the pain. If you do, you will always be angry, overly sensitive, and wary of other men or deep relationships.

Learn forgiveness. What is forgiveness? What is not true forgiveness? Are there levels of forgiveness? Sometimes forgiveness is thought to be a quick, one-time action. In reality, it's better to see it as leaves in a head of lettuce, with layer after layer to be peeled off.

Forgiveness is not ignoring the hurt or denying that it happened. It is not saying, "I will not think or feel the pain." True forgiveness can be accomplished only when you recognize that you have been violated. In a sense, all the emotions we encouraged you to think about during the shock stage are necessary for you to genuinely forgive someone. Grieving over your losses will also help you forgive. Proper mourning is an important early element of the forgiving process.

What does forgiveness mean? Let's clear the air on several things. To forgive does not at all suggest that

☐ the other person was not wrong

☐ it really was only a small matter after all

☐ he can't be blamed for his weaknesses

☐ a few words of apology will erase the feelings from a long-standing problem

☐ he didn't know what he was doing

☐ I caused him to act or react that way[2]

Therefore, forgiveness does not mean that the dreadful abandonment never happened. Nor does it mean that it was not wrong. Instead, forgiveness is a sense of releasing this person to God.

As you begin to think about the implications of forgiveness, you're also going to ask yourself, *Can I forgive myself? Can I forgive other people who contributed to this abandonment?* (such as Jennifer in Bob and Ann's situation). Eventually you may have to face the question, *Can I forgive God?* At this stage in your healing process, you may find yourself silently bearing a grudge against God: *With all of his power, why did he let this happen?*

Extend grace. To fully move to acceptance, you will have to grant your husband a "grace forgiveness." A grace forgiveness is something that you give to a person not because he is worthy, not because he has asked for forgiveness, not because the situation has been corrected, but because God has forgiven you and he wants you to extend that forgiveness to someone else.

Holding a grudge keeps all of your pain and anger bottled up inside of you. It prevents you from moving to acceptance. The only way to get to acceptance without incorporating forgiveness is to deny your feelings. Sooner or later those denied feelings of pain will burst out in explosions at yourself, your children or your friends.

Forgiveness allows you to ventilate those feelings. It allows you to release them to someone else—to God. Then God can work in your mind and emotions, freeing you up to move on to acceptance.

Ann was having a great deal of difficulty coming to the point of forgiving Bob. She had gone through all of the processes in leading up to forgiveness, but she could not actually step across that line to forgive Bob.

At that point, I (Jim) shared with Ann my own struggle in forgiving my father. I had told my father I would be willing to forgive him if he would only ask, if he would say he was sorry. He just sat there and said nothing. I kept reasoning, *Why should I forgive him when he doesn't ask? Why should I do more than God does?* The Bible says that when we confess our sins, God forgives us (1 Jn 1:9). Even God doesn't forgive us until we ask.

My father's terrible offenses against our family drove a deep wedge of mistrust, accusation and fear between us, our children, our grandchildren and many of our extended family members. The pain in each of us was very intense. I was absolutely unwilling to forgive my father for this terrible, permanent damage he had caused to each family member.

After about six years of not forgiving my father, I finally told God that I believed my father would never ask for forgiveness and, ultimately, I would have to forgive him after he died. That stage continued for two more years.

Finally, one night at a national men's conference, I sat in the front row, enjoying the music before I was to get up to speak. In that setting, God spoke quite clearly to me and said, "Jim, if you are willing to forgive your father after he dies, why don't you do it now and release your emotions and your heart from all this pain?" As I sat there, I could finally say, "God, I forgive him now!"

During the last session of the conference, I challenged the men also to deal with the past pain of their lives, to forgive the people that needed to be forgiven and to ask for forgiveness if necessary. In short, I challenged them to sweep away the debris of unforgiveness that had gathered.

Then I asked the men to write their commitments on pieces of paper. These symbols of pain were gathered, put in wastebaskets and burned. Together we were turning over our pain and hurts to God with a sense of relief—with a sense of commitment.

On my slip of paper I wrote, "I forgive my father for his terrible offenses against our whole family, and I release him entirely into the hands of God. The matter is no longer mine, but God's."

Pressure lifted off my whole personality. It had been eight years, and it was time. Forgiveness finally was the most normal and correct thing for me to do.

We don't want you to be pressured to be on anyone else's time schedule for when you will grant your husband a grace forgiveness. But when the right time comes, and when you give him that forgiveness as your gift, you will also receive a gift from God. Your heart will be healed.

Withholding forgiveness is not going to harm your husband as much as yourself. The more quickly you'll realize that God wants you to let him help you with this problem, the more quickly you will be moving to acceptance.

Forgiveness doesn't mean that you trust your husband or that all is back to normal. Trust is learned *and* earned. Forgiveness is not about trust—it's about releasing your pain. Trust grows only as the other person becomes trustworthy. God doesn't ask us to trust a person who has violated us—we are only to forgive.

Burn your paper slips of pain. Months before, we had asked Ann to write down her feelings of anger, rage, sadness, fear, shame, guilt—everything associated with her response to Bob's abandonment. By this time she had dozens and dozens of paper slips detailing her emotions.

We asked Ann to invite her supportive friends to her home to help her in a ceremony of releasing her pain to God. Each friend was asked to bring a Bible reading about God's care, God's help in the time of trouble or how God wants us to cast all our concerns and anxieties on him.

As the friends gathered, they each reassured Ann of how much they loved her and believed God wanted to heal her. Then, one by one, they read from the Bible, sharing what the section meant to them and what they felt it could mean to Ann.

Earlier Ann had started a fire in her fireplace. After her friends had shared their Scripture selections, she took a seat next to the fire and read the feelings she had been writing down for months. After she had finished reading, she jammed the slips into a small paper bag, rolled it up tightly and threw it into the fireplace.

It was a very touching moment as the group held hands and watched Ann's released anxiety be surrendered to God. Her pain was burned up, symbolically, and carried away by God's love and care.

Hold a symbolic burial. Then Ann got up and put one more chair into the circle of friends. On that chair she placed her favorite picture of Bob.

Then, talking to the picture as if she were talking to Bob, she said, "Bob, I forgive you for what has happened. I release you totally to God."

Then she said, "Jesus, I give Bob and Jennifer to you, along with all my pain. I know I cannot forget what has taken place, but I cannot live with the pain. I release all of this to you. I ask only that I may be able to sense your deep peace that assures me you understand and will continue to help me through this process."

When Ann finished praying, each of the friends prayed for her, for the children, and for Bob and Jennifer. They prayed for God to work good out of evil, to give "beauty for ashes" and "joy instead of mourning," as Isaiah 61:3 promises.

When the group had finished praying, Ann went over to the chair, slipped the photo out of the frame, walked to the fireplace and placed the photo in the flames. Symbolically, Ann laid Bob and their marriage to rest—as in death.

Promises of hope. Ann asked each of her friends to write out their Bible verses on small cards so she could place them in strategic places to remind her of God's love. And she asked them to put their names at the bottom, so she could remember their special gift of love. She put these new cards of hope in conspicuous places: her bathroom mirror, the refrigerator door, the table where her TV control sat, her checkbook, the dashboard of her car. She tried to always carry one of them in her purse or pocket.

Ann was experiencing the great spiritual change that takes place as a person moves from pain to acceptance. She wasn't able to say exactly when it began, but it was like the wave in the ocean. She knew it was moving toward shore. She knew it had great power. But it wasn't until the wave started to rise up, curl over and finally crash on the beach that she realized the great power of God as the healer. He was the one giving her acceptance of Bob's abandonment and hope for her future.

Blessed is the Lord, for he has shown me that his never-failing love protects me like the walls of a fort! I spoke too hastily when I said, "The Lord has deserted me," for you listened to my plea and answered me. (Ps 31:21-22)

— Part Four —

Rebuilding Your Life

When you have wrestled with the unwanted changes and finally accepted your new life situation, it is time to start rebuilding. You've already taken some steps—you had no choice. But thinking through wise choices will help you avoid mistakes.

Many women who have gone through the shock and despair of a marriage breakup are now living happy and fulfilled lives. Not the lives they had planned, but lives that are often, in some respects, *better* than before.

No one can rob you of your personhood—unless you allow it. People have come through rape, concentration camp, racial oppression, all sorts of horrible experiences that might have destroyed them—and come out standing tall, because *they knew who they were.*

Your personhood has been threatened because of the stigma of abandonment and divorce; you have been misunderstood by some people whose respect is important to you; worst of all, the one person whose respect and love you treasured most has communicated, "I no longer value you," or "You are not a desirable woman," or "You are a disappointment."

Remember, though, that other people do love and respect you. And God says to you, "You are precious to me and honored, and I love you" (Is 43:4). You can come through this tragic circumstance with your personhood intact and growing stronger!

Now you are ready for *reconstruction*. You will still have feelings and tasks to deal with.

☐ *Feelings:* You are in charge! God is with you! You have more confidence as you begin rebuilding your life.

☐ *Tasks:* Patiently, yet persistently, work through the reconstruction steps and time frames related to legal issues, money and work, children, selfhood, dating and sex.

As you grow in your new identity, you will cease to be simply a wife whose husband rejected her. You have other roles in which you can be successful. You are a priceless human being.

The chapters in this section will take a close look at five important areas to consider as you begin to rebuild: legal issues, money and work, children, selfhood, dating and sex.

—10—

Legal Issues

*T*HE INTERCOM BUZZED. MY SECRETARY SAID THAT ANN WAS ON THE phone, wanting an immediate appointment. I already had a full schedule for the day, but I told the secretary to tell her I'd be willing to see her for about twenty minutes at 5:15 that afternoon.

The secretary said that Ann was raging, almost out of control, about something that Bob had done. The hours she had to wait did not calm her down very much. She hardly was seated in my office when she exploded.

"Bob is the most gutless person I have ever seen! Not only did he walk out on me and the children—he doesn't have the guts to face me.

"He has violated everything he said he believed about marriage and family. Everybody's mad at him—his parents, my parents, all of our friends, the people at church, the Thursday night dinner group. We're all furious with him *and* with Jennifer.

"Earlier I thought maybe she seduced him. Maybe she just kept waving that hot little body around in front of him. But then I came to believe, 'No, he made a choice—a deliberate choice of Jennifer over me.' Now the gutless little weasel isn't enough of a man to face me. He has to get somebody else to do it."

Ann took the oversized brown envelope in her lap and started beating it on my desk and yelling, "I hate him, I hate him, I hate him!" Then she broke into uncontrolled crying, her body convulsing with sobs as she asked, "Why, why, why?" I could do nothing at this point but let all the vile green bile of anguish pour out of her system.

Her mood kept changing from violent explosions of anger to frenzied sobbing, amid the repeated questions, "Why did this happen to me and my children? Where was God? Why didn't I see this coming? Why didn't someone warn me that our marriage was about to break up?"

The secretary had clearly told Ann that she would have only twenty minutes, but at the twenty-minute mark, I still had not found out what had happened. Finally, after the repeated cycles of rage, sobbing and questioning began to slow down, I asked, "Tell me, Ann, what happened?"

It was as if I had thrown a lighted match into a can of gasoline. She exploded again, calling Bob a gutless weasel. But this time she followed it up with, "He didn't have the nerve to face me and hand me the divorce papers; he had them delivered by a special messenger.

"Can you imagine how humiliating it is to sign for the delivery of your own divorce papers—to be alone, no one to talk to, no one to comfort you? Somebody ought to teach a course on how to handle it when the special messenger brings your divorce papers from your gutless husband."

Now Ann started to joke: "I know, we can get that little weasel to teach a course. Wouldn't that be a riot? Mr. Perfect, Mr.

Holy-Joe, teaching people 'How to Give Your Wife the Shaft.'

"Well, what am I to do now? I've never even touched legal papers before. Sure, I signed papers when we bought our house, but Bob and the lawyer handled all that legal mumbo-jumbo."

Then she jumped up from her chair and leaned over the desk. "Look at this junk, look at it. Look at this paragraph where it says I'm a rotten wife! Then look over here, they've got it all figured out! Who gets what, when Bob can visit the children, who gets to keep which car. They've also decided that I need to sell the house and move somewhere else!

"They've made all of these decisions and I've not talked a minute to either of them! I wish I could go over to that lawyer's office and blow up the place. That's it, maybe I could hire somebody to burn it down, then set a bomb in Bob's car so that when he and Little Miss Hot Pants get in, the thing will blow up."

Again Ann began to sob and sob. "What am I supposed to do with these papers? Nobody ever prepared me for this. But more than that, what am I supposed to do with all of this anger? I hate him! Do you understand? *I hate him!*"

Now Ann had a vicious look on her face. Her eyes flashed and her jaw was set. I could see her hands trembling with rage.

By this time it was 6:05. I had to get home to eat, change clothes and be prepared for a 7:30 meeting. So I said, "Ann, I realize that you're in a great deal of pain. You're confused. You feel exploited and totally unprepared for what's happening. I want you to know that I care very deeply for you and what's going on, but you also need to know that we must stop our session now.

"Before we leave, I want to remind you that God is not surprised by what's happened. He's going to give you the encouragement you need. These are very, very painful problems. Not only is God going to help you, but Sally and I are also going to be alongside as you work through this whole legal hassle.

Even though it's late, I want to pray with you before you go. And be sure to see your lawyer tomorrow, if possible."

Ann had been in touch with her lawyer all along, and he had warned her that the divorce papers might upset her. She knew these were coming, but seeing the papers produced more anger than she had expected.

Ann was somewhat calmer. I walked around to the front of the desk and she stood up. I placed my hand on her shoulder and prayed, asking God to give her his wisdom and comfort during these very difficult hours. I encouraged Ann that tomorrow her lawyer would help her with these legal issues and help her walk through this painful period.

Remember that each woman's situation will be very different, so our comments here will be general to give an overall picture. Our purpose is not to replace your lawyer. You must get exact information from your lawyer about how to proceed. Our ideas are only suggestions and general information to guide you to some of the questions you need to ask.

If you have some experience with legal and financial matters or have worked in those fields, this area will not be as threatening to you. If you're like Ann, tell your lawyer frankly, "I don't even know the questions to ask. Please start from zero." If he or she is competent, you will get understandable explanations.

Let's look at some of the general legal issues that you will probably face.

Choosing a Lawyer

When do I first contact a lawyer? When your husband moves out, you should have your first discussion with a lawyer to learn what to watch for, what your rights are and how to protect your children. You generally won't take any legal actions at this point, but you have established a source for legal help in case you do need it.

Where do I find a lawyer? Talk to your pastor, to your counselor if you're seeing one, to a few family friends. Most of all, talk to women who have gone through a divorce. These women will probably be able to warn you to avoid certain incompetent lawyers as well as recommend some helpful ones. As you talk to several people, you may notice two or three lawyers mentioned over and over again. These are the ones to interview when choosing your own lawyer. Plan to interview two or three candidates. This will give you the opportunity to see their overall philosophy and how well they communicate with you. Then you can choose the most qualified lawyer and the one who will best work with you.

Who pays the lawyer's bill? The final divorce decree will stipulate that your husband is to pay all legal costs. Don't you do it. He wants the divorce—let him pay. You may need to pay a small fee to get the process started. This can be refunded to you later.

What type of lawyer do I want? Obviously, you want a person who is knowledgeable about divorce. But as you're choosing a lawyer, you want something more than just divorce knowledge. Let's look at additional characteristics:

1. Choose a lawyer with whom you feel comfortable. For the next months you're going to be working closely together. You need to feel that he or she is helping you. But don't confuse your lawyer with a counselor or your close friends. You should find warmth and comfort elsewhere; you hire your lawyer to work for you in a business arrangement.

2. Choose a lawyer who will work with you to attempt a reconciliation, not just press full steam ahead toward a divorce. It's appropriate to ask what his or her attitude is toward reconciliation. Ask for referrals to couples the lawyer has helped get back together. If the lawyer cannot give you the names of any couples, perhaps he or she is not the one for you.

3. Choose a lawyer who is willing to play the delaying game. Sometimes marriages can be saved if a lawyer will use all the delaying tactics available in your state. Saving the marriage should be the first goal.

4. Choose a lawyer who will be on your side. Most people assume that a lawyer will take their side. But we have met lawyers who are so conciliatory that when it's time to negotiate the settlement, they do not fight for their client's right to an appropriate financial settlement. They give away the store. Don't be embarrassed to ask your divorced friends what kind of settlement they got. If it was a low settlement or caused a great deal of family disruption, look for a different lawyer.

5. Choose a lawyer with a proven record of protecting the client's assets while the separation and divorce are taking place. Sometimes an unscrupulous husband will transfer all financial assets into hidden bank accounts so that when it comes time to divide the estate, very little is left. Your lawyer should protect you in this transition time.

How do I protect my assets and get immediate cash? Your lawyer should be the primary person for this kind of advice. Here are some areas that you'll want to talk about with him or her.

1. How do I get my husband to keep paying the bills during this separation and divorce transition time?

2. Are there any of our assets that I could draw against or liquidate to raise immediate cash?

3. Do I need to seize any assets to keep them from disappearing? Very early in the separation you may need to draw out money from the checking and savings accounts and transfer it to your own personal accounts in order to keep your husband from emptying the joint accounts.

4. Should I get my own charge cards and drop my name from any joint charge cards? Your lawyer may counsel you to do this as soon as it is possible. He or she may also file a legal notice in

the paper, disclaiming any bills created solely by your husband. Getting your own charge cards and credit accounts will begin to build your individual credit for the future if you need to buy a car or a house.

5. Should I consider welfare? We consulted with a lawyer about some of the legal aspects for an abandoned woman. One of his very first remarks was, "As soon as a husband files divorce papers, the wife should start the process of getting on welfare if her income is low enough."

The problem is that welfare has a stigma attached to it. Many people do not want to be known as using welfare, nor do they want to go through the humiliating process of seeking welfare approval. As a result, many abandoned women do not think of welfare until they become terribly, terribly desperate. But our lawyer friend's advice was to get started with the welfare applications immediately, because it takes a long time before the woman actually sees any money from that source.

Every woman's case is unique. It would be inappropriate to take some of the more drastic steps we've listed if there appears to be a high likelihood of the marriage being reconciled. It's difficult for the woman caught in the early stages of abandonment to make an appropriate estimation of whether she should take these extreme steps or not. Legal advice is very helpful at this early stage, assuming that you have a lawyer who will protect your rights.

No-Fault Divorce

A number of states have a type of divorce called no-fault: one where the lawyers and the court do not try to fix blame on either partner. The focus is on the negotiated settlement. State laws vary, but typically a no-fault divorce can be concluded in a short period of time, from one month to a few months. The intention of this legislation is to eliminate some of the divorce costs and delays.

141

Unfortunately, sometimes a divorce is rushed through so rapidly that the people hardly realize what's happening. These fast divorces don't allow time for people to take a second look at whether this marriage has the possibility of reconciliation.

The Divorce Papers

To most abandoned women, it isn't the divorce papers that frighten them—it's what they mean! Therefore, most abandoned women react *very* negatively when they first see these papers.

Typically, divorce papers are about eight by fourteen inches, held together in a colored binder that makes them look attractive and official. But inside the cover, the woman is confronted with coldness, matter-of-factness and a new language called "legalese."

Take these papers to your lawyer as soon as possible. He or she can best explain the implications for you and your children for the years to come. These papers are worth understanding. We know that you're very angry, but your anger isn't going to make the divorce papers go away. It's better to learn how to work within the system to protect your rights and your children's.

Remember that the divorce papers you receive have been drawn up by your husband's lawyer—to protect your husband and to get as much as possible for him. Your husband's lawyer often is *not on your side.* To put it bluntly, he may be very willing to exploit you and the children in order to get more for your husband. On the other hand, both lawyers may seek only the best for all parties.

When you get these papers, don't be shocked, as Ann was, thinking that all of the decisions are already made. Nothing is final until you sign. Plan not to sign them until you feel sure you've gotten the best terms possible. These papers are simply a notification that your husband wants a divorce. They also lay down his general guidelines for what he and his lawyer think the settlement should be. You won't be signing them into effect until after a lot of discussion!

Negotiating the Settlement

The divorce decree has several parts to it. One part legally divorces the two of you as a married couple. Generally, that is a very small part of the decree. The bigger parts are the agreements on how you're going to divide your possessions and arrange the care and custody of your children.

1. Maintenance. Some agreements include maintenance (the amount of money paid either in a lump sum or in payments to the wife for her personal support). These days judges are less likely to award maintenance; because many women work, husbands can get by without paying this. The husband's lawyer will argue that she doesn't need that kind of support. But if a woman has primarily been a homemaker, she may need support, including medical insurance.

2. Splitting up the net worth. The general rule of thumb is that each of the partners gets fifty percent of their combined net assets (after all bills are paid).

Look at this section of the papers very closely. Help your lawyer identify everything that you own—anything that has worth. Your lawyer will guide you to identify as much of your total assets as you possibly can. Then you and your lawyer will assign a general dollar figure that sums up the combined assets of you and your husband.

A great deal of opportunity for negotiation arises as you come to splitting up your assets. Don't be embarrassed to press for more. This is probably the last shot you're going to get to financially provide for your children, so be *very tough*. The general rule is to ask for more than you know you'll get. Then you'll be able to negotiate from a position of strength.

Start from the premise, "I want it all. I'm not the one who

wants the divorce. If we were still married, the kids and I would not have to experience a reduced lifestyle, so why should we put up with it now? You're the one who wants to leave."

One woman told us she made a private list, to help her clarify her thinking. She put her assets into three categories:

1. Absolutely must have—will not yield at all in these areas.
2. Nice to have, but not absolutely necessary.
3. Bargaining items or issues.

This woman was able to get custody of her children. Plus, the kids were never to sleep at Dad's house or be exposed to his drinking buddies or his family. By giving him the stereo, all the CDs and the living-room furniture, she felt she had traded moral value for less valuable items. For her, that was a great trade.

Don't overlook the fact of your husband's future earnings. If you worked to put him through school or some kind of training program, your efforts have provided him with the ability to earn a higher level of income *all of his life*. You have a right to tap into some of that income. You may get a 60-40 split in your favor rather than just a 50-50 split of current assets.

Your right to future income might give you the bargaining leverage to get more of the current net worth. You can't predict what's going to happen to your husband in the future, so it would be better to get all that you can now, rather than counting on him to give you so much a month in the future. Settlements that include future payments from your husband tend to become sources of irritation. So try to take the whole estate now rather than to depend on your husband's "dole" in the future.

What About the Children?

1. Child custody. Which parent will have control of the child's life? In the past, almost every case was decided in favor of the mother. But more cases are now being won by fathers who become the child's custodian because the mother is declared unfit. Sometimes couples agree to a 50-50 split of a child's time. Sadly, the focus of custody often is on the wishes and needs of the parents rather than on the best situation for the child.

Children do better when they are not being bounced back and forth between parents. Help them have a stable, nourishing environment. Even if there is joint custody, it can sometimes be arranged for the children to sleep in their own bed every night, minimizing the disturbance of the kids' routine.

2. Child support. How much will your husband pay to support the children for the future? The questions to be ironed out are: the amount of money, whether it is a lump sum or a monthly payment, at what age the children will no longer receive their father's support, whether the children will be on their father's medical plan, and whether the father will provide any future educational funds.

As you work toward a child support agreement, remember to start high, making many demands. You can always settle for less, but it's difficult to ask for $500 a month after having first asked for only $250 a month. Some states use a flat percentage, which can eliminate arguing and also provide for continued escalation of support without your going back to court.

The rule of thumb is to get as much money as possible now, in cash or in trust accounts, so you don't have a running battle in years to come. At this stage in the negotiation, your husband wants out of the marriage. He is more willing to make concessions now than he will be five years down the road.

Another problem with ongoing payments is that frequently the ex-husband shows up at the door to give the wife the check. This process means repeated humiliation for both people. It's better to set up a bank account where these support checks can be deposited. The understanding should be that if the checks are not deposited on time, you will not call your husband—your lawyer will contact him. Another possibility is to have funds "direct-deposited" from the husband's paycheck. Now you are out of the nagging loop of continually begging your husband to pay on time or hearing a nasty remark when he hands you the check.

3. Child visitation. Prepare to be flexible. Your husband will soon become your ex-husband, but he will always be the father of your children. A little later in the book, we'll be discussing the child issue in more depth, but for now, realize that your husband does have legal rights and you both need to be flexible to accommodate each other.

Don't allow visitation rights to become a continual battle-ground. If he is late picking them up or dropping them off, be tolerant. In return, he needs to be tolerant if you don't have the kids ready quite on time.

As you negotiate the settlement, you need to spell out as clearly as possible what the visitation rights will be. The more clearly everyone understands the agreement, the easier it will be to comply and, if necessary, to enforce.

Other Painful Issues
Court appearance. Our court system is set up so that two lawyers vigorously argue for the rights of their parties. Then a judge makes the decision that will be the final decree. Typically, the two lawyers try to hammer out all disagreements ahead of time and come to a fair compromise, so they present a unified front to the court. The action of the court, then, is to ratify this decree as a fact.

If you and your husband have a great deal of disagreement or are in an out-and-out legal fight, more courtroom drama will take place. Nevertheless, most of the arguing will be done by the lawyers, not by you. In some cases, you may be called to testify. Your lawyer has been through this experience many times, and he or she will coach you about what is likely to happen and the kinds of questions you might be asked.

An important tip from one divorced woman: plan a lunch or dinner with a few of your closest friends on the day of your last court appearance—and again the day your divorce is final. Your friends will be the boost you need at this sad, emotionally confusing time.

Coping with your ex-husband and his new wife. Keep in mind that your goal with the legal issues is to solve as many problems as possible at the time of the divorce rather than letting them drag on. All carry-over issues present opportunities for more conflict.

For example, suppose that the settlement says you are permitted to live in the house for one year. Then you're to sell it, and half of the proceeds are to go to your ex-husband. Suppose that housing prices fall drastically during the year. Do you sell the house and take a twenty-five percent loss, or do you try to make an agreement with your ex-husband to ride out the price drop for a few more years, waiting to sell it at a better price?

If you sell the house at the end of the year, you may find yourself in a lawsuit with the new wife. She could charge that you didn't maintain the house properly and poor maintenance is the reason it lost property value. She may pressure your ex-husband into suing you for many thousands of dollars to compensate for the loss.

Hundreds of scenarios could be imagined that can provide minor or major conflict between you and your ex-husband. Keep in mind that the goal is to make the break as clean as possible so that few, if any, long-term issues are carried over.

Remember God

The legal and financial issues may seem overwhelming. In those moments, remember God. He will give you the peace you need, guide you to the right people for help and point you to the right place to step as you navigate these treacherous waters.

Think of yourself as crossing a stream—jumping from rock to rock. God is giving you the wisdom to choose the right rock to jump to and courage to make that next leap. Ultimately, you'll get to the other side of the stream—and beyond your divorce.

When you wonder where to jump next, remember God—he won't let you mess up. Ultimately, all things work together for good.

I weep with grief; my heart is heavy with sorrow; encourage and cheer me with your words. Keep me far from every wrong; help me, undeserving as I am, to obey your laws, for I have chosen to do right. I cling to your commands and follow them as closely as I can. Lord, don't let me make a mess of things. If you will only help me to want your will, then I will follow your laws even more closely. (Ps 119:28-32)

—11—

Money
and Work

*I*N THE FIRST WEEK AFTER BOB HAD LEFT ANN, BILLS BEGAN ARRIVING. When she finally got up her courage and opened them, Ann realized she was facing a major financial crisis. Bob had not made any contact with her, nor had he sent any money.

Ann had a part-time job so she could be there when the kids got home from school. She earned about one-third of what Bob earned. When Bob moved out, the expenses didn't suddenly drop. The only difference Ann noticed was that Bob had made his car payment sometime during the month; otherwise, all of the other costs were the same.

The average family is only about three weeks away from financial chaos. Ann was a little bit better off because she had a job and also money in savings and checking accounts. In addition, she also had a large network of family and friends who could help if things got really bad, though she was hesitant at the thought of having to ask. Many abandoned women do not have Ann's resources. Typically, when a husband abandons the home, the family's income drops below the poverty level.

Since many abandoning husbands do not support the family until forced by the courts, the most desperate women are those who have chosen to be a wife and mother only and do not have an additional career. They generally have no immediate income, and because they've been out of the career market so long, it's difficult for them to find a job to support the family.

Not only are you facing terrible financial stress that you didn't ask for, but the situation is a continuous reminder of the loss of your marriage. Each bill, each financial sacrifice, each reduction in lifestyle is also a blow to your self-image. You will feel better about yourself as you begin to take charge of your financial situation.

Taking Control of Your Finances

1. *Focus on "what is."* Don't waste your emotional energy on wishing that life was different or hoping that your husband eventually will feel responsible to care for the family's financial needs. The *what is* of life is that you have been abandoned as a wife, and that means you have also been financially abandoned.

If you are to have enough money to pay the bills, you're going to have to take drastic measures. Perhaps you'll even have to do some uncomfortable things, such as legally forcing your husband to provide funds for the family, asking friends for help or going on welfare. If so, realize that there is no shame in doing what is right and necessary and also that this a temporary circumstance; you *will* get on your feet eventually.

2. *Look at the two ways to control your finances—increasing income and reducing spending.* There are no other options. If you act quickly in both of these areas, you can keep the crisis from becoming worse and slowly begin to recover financially.

Take a very hard look at the money coming in and going out. List ways you can spend less—small economy moves and also more drastic actions to take if it proves necessary. Then list any ways you can think of in which you could bring in even a few dollars. This chapter will give you some suggestions in both areas.

3. Don't waste time viewing yourself as a victim. You and your children truly are victims, but encourage your children to see the positive aspects of this painful time. Depending on your children's ages, maybe their money-saving sacrifices will give them a new understanding of poor people around the world who go without many things your kids continue to enjoy.

In some countries, large groups of people are at the point of starvation. For them, it's not a choice of eating out or ordering in a pizza tonight. They can't rent a video, go to Disneyland, drive to the beach for a picnic or pay for swimming lessons. For them the problem is, "Where can we find *any* food to eat today?" Remembering those who have less—and sometimes sharing with them in some way—helps prevent the growth of dissatisfaction and self-pity in our own hearts.

4. Remember that God knows and God cares. Perhaps at this point you're tempted to throw this book across the room. When you get done being angry, remember that God *does know* and he *does care.* He knows life on this planet isn't fair. He knows you are in a hard time. And he offers comfort and help.

We encouraged Ann to strengthen her relationship with God, focusing on his promises and care. "Ann, tell God frankly that the situation seems impossible. Tell him you don't know how it's going to work out; ask him to do whatever changing and miracles are necessary so you will survive as a family."

God did intervene in Ann's situation in a number of ways. Bob started to send some financial help after Ann's lawyer coached her on how to ask. Ann's parents jumped in with additional financial help. Once the kids understood the circumstances, they were willing to cut costs, and Ann was given the courage she needed to face a temporarily reduced lifestyle.

Ann worked for months on the issues of money and her job. She focused on the two major areas as she attempted to get her chaotic financial situation under control: *income* from all sources, both long-term and short-term, and *spending* for the right things. It's necessary to face these issues in the short term, before divorce, as well as in the long term, after divorce.

Income
Paying the bills short-term. Toughness is the key to paying the bills that are due immediately. The following suggestions might keep you from being swamped by the financial overload:

1. If you are working, keep your job. Even though the emotional pressure some days is overwhelming, you must not give up. You must not let the circumstances of life whip you. You're a valuable person. So in order to keep the financial chaos from overtaking you, keep your job.

2. Find new ways to bring in some dollars. Some women make crafts for a nearby shop, do alterations for a dry cleaner or department store, or do payroll work for two evenings at the end of each month. Moms with small children may be able to take in another child for a working friend. Look for ways to turn a few hours into extra income.

3. Appeal to your husband for support. It's best to approach your husband in terms of his helping the children, not providing a place for *you* to live. Remind him that the kids need a stable home, food, clothes and a car to get to their activities. It's bad for the children that the marriage is breaking up; it will be even more tragic if they have to move or get along with less than their friends have.

4. Be tough enough to go after your husband legally if he doesn't respond to your verbal appeal. Ask your lawyer to advise you on the best steps to take if you get no cooperation and need to take legal action.

5. *Consider borrowing from friends or family members.* The legal help might not happen quickly enough to be able to pay the current bills. We know that asking requires swallowing your pride, but it's better than being evicted from your house. Also, you might be able to borrow against insurance, get a home equity loan on your house or get a loan against some other asset you own. It might help your husband realize his responsibility if you can tell him what you plan to do—he might be embarrassed enough to help.

6. *Sell things.* Maybe it's time to have a garage sale. You might raise $200 to $500 for immediate bills. A garage sale is also a good way to get the kids to realize the depth of the crisis. Help them understand that the money earned from the garage sale is going to buy groceries for the coming week or two, pay for their lessons or cover a trip to visit the grandparents. Ask them to suggest things to get rid of to raise necessary cash. We're not saying that kids should be asked to bear adult burdens, but involve them—because they *are* involved.

7. *Go on welfare.* While this is a last resort that no one likes to turn to, you may need the help temporarily. Don't wait until you're desperate.

8. *Allow people to help you.* Most people will make remarks such as, "We are so sorry that your husband has abandoned you. If we can do anything, please let us know." Don't respond by simply saying, "Thank you." Tell them your needs.

Say, "Thank you. Yes, you *can* help with some things. I'm going through a really tough financial time right now. My husband is unwilling to help financially. The legal process is taking a long time. I've applied for some welfare help, but, frankly, I need some short-term financial help to get through these next few weeks. Thanks for asking—and thanks for any help you can give to the kids and me."

Many churches have special funds to help people in emergencies. We know it takes nerve, but ask your pastor or a church leader if you might benefit from the fund until you get on your feet. Or you could ask a friend to ask the church for you.

Your financial situation is going to demand toughness, but don't cop out. God needs a good woman like you in the world. If all the good people decided to jump ship when the going gets rough, the world would be left to the scoundrels. Keep focused, and keep remembering that God knows and cares, and *he is working in your life.*

Paying the bills long-term. The long-term solution is to increase your income. You've already done the short-term cutting of expenses. Some long-term increase in income will probably come as the court forces your husband to pay child support. But remember, one of our national tragedies is that many fathers refuse to pay the court-directed financial support. To depend on your husband to provide the long-term finances is probably a bad miscalculation. Then there is the question you'll face later: "Who will pay the bills after the children reach age eighteen?"

Ultimately, you're going to need a job—a good job. So the question is, how do you get a good job? A minimum-wage job is not going to provide for you and your children. The way up the job ladder is through education and training. You need to have skills and credentials that will open the door to more money.

For example, if you were a secretary before you were married, you may not have used computers for word processing. Most offices now expect a person they hire to have basic computer word-processing skills. If you can only use a typewriter, your job opportunities will be few and your income will be very low. The answer is to take a few evening classes in word processing.

In some fields, such as nursing, dental technology or counseling, you will need state or national certification. Even if you've finished all your training but don't have your certification, you're still going to end up with a low-paying intern-type job. The answer is to make sure you get your credentials.

Friends are a good source to steer you to better-paying jobs. They know your skills and abilities and can counsel you on jobs that perhaps you've not considered. They can also introduce you to strategic people who may have influence for hiring. Learn to use the networks at church, in your small groups, where you are currently working or even in your neighborhood to connect you with job possibilities.

An employment agency may also be a help to you. Two basic types of agencies are available. One collects a fee from you for its services; the other agency collects the fee from the employer. Typically, the fee for finding you a job is the first month's salary. Since you are already scraping the bottom of the financial barrel, try to find an employment agency that asks the employer to pay the fee—not you.

An employment agency can also help you to develop an effective résumé. As you go to a job interview, you'll not only look capable, but you'll have a professional document to leave with them as they make the decision on which person to employ.

Try to find a job that's not a dead-end street. Does the company offer to pay for on-the-job or off-site training? The basic question is, "Will this job allow me to develop my skills, to grow as a person and to enjoy increased financial income?"

Spending

Remember the basic principle to keep from financial chaos: you have to increase income and/or decrease spending. It's time to think *simplified lifestyle*.

As you begin to plan how to spend your money in your new

circumstances, ask yourself, "Is it possible not to spend *any* money?" Now, after you finish laughing hysterically, think about that question awhile. As you go through every area of your budget, ask yourself, *Is there some way not to spend any money in this area?*

When you plan your spending, list the major areas, such as housing, utilities, automobile, food and household supplies, clothes, services (dry cleaning, haircuts, dentist), school costs, gifts for relatives, charitable giving, recreation and so on.

You may add other items to your list, but the point is—make a list. Ask yourself, *What percentage do I need to reduce spending to make ends meet?* Suppose you need to cut twenty-five percent. After each item, list as accurately as possible what you are currently spending in that area. In a second column, write down a dollar number that is twenty-five percent less than you are currently spending.

Now comes the *real* task: reducing your current budget by twenty-five percent. Remember, the only other option is to increase the income. Let's take a whack at developing a tight budget.

Housing. If you can get your husband to cover the mortgage, including taxes and insurance, then you are basically left with only utilities and maintenance. For now, eliminate all preventative maintenance. Do only emergency maintenance, and use your network of family and friends to cover these areas. Whenever a friend fixes something, watch so you'll learn how to do it yourself for a future time.

If your husband does not help with the mortgage, you probably will need to plan on less expensive housing. This is an emotional issue, because it often means a change of neighborhood and schools. But first use your lawyer to put pressure on your husband.

The next major area is utilities. Ask some of your friends how they would cut corners in this area. Then sit down with your kids and ask them to suggest cuts to make. Kids' suggestions will vary according to their age, but it's important to let them know you value this opinion. Maybe you'll come up with some items such as these:

☐ Stop watering the lawn.

☐ Drop cable TV.

☐ Eliminate the second phone line and all extras other than the basic service.

☐ Wash dishes and clothes less frequently and in bigger loads.

☐ Don't run the furnace or the air conditioner unless absolutely desperate.

☐ Fill only the first cup of your dishwasher with detergent.

☐ Turn out unnecessary lights.

You may think of lots of ways to cut costs if you start from the question "Is it possible not to spend *anything* for this?" and then work up. Sometime later you'll be able to add a few of these extras again, but for now you need to survive.

Automobile. Would it be possible to get along without using the car? Could you temporarily use public transportation or carpool? Perhaps the kids could use their bicycles more. If you should happen to have more than one car, is it possible to sell one to raise immediate cash? If you can survive by using public transportation, sell the car to raise immediate cash and to cut your insurance, maintenance and fuel expenses. If you must keep your car, ask for your insurance agent's counsel about temporarily reducing coverage as much as possible.

Clothing. Again, the basic question is, "Do I have to spend anything?" Delay clothing purchases for now; at a later time you may have more money. Also, don't take your clothes to the cleaners as often. Let them air out in a breezy room between wearings and try some spot cleaning. In some communities, elementary schools have great twice-a-year sales of children's clothing in good condition. Some "second time around" shops hold real bargains if you can find time to explore them.

Services. We are a service-oriented society. Look at every area of your budget where you are paying someone to do a service for you. Ask, "Do I have to spend money in this area? Can I delay services, barter services with someone else or do it myself? Or can someone in my network of friends and family members help me?"

Lifestyle. Do you have to spend any money in this area? Do you need to eat out, get your nails done, attend a charity dinner? Do you need to rent videos or buy CDs, more makeup or new clothes? Can you eliminate a vacation, or can you change it to a no-cost-stay-at-home-free-museum-and-park vacation? Sometimes the answer is no; a video will cost less than a visit to the movie theater, or the kids really want to eat at Pizza World—but you can do it less often.

Remember to use your network of friends to help you as you plan the budget. Get their coaching. Look in the library for books on budgeting and simplifying your lifestyle. And remember the key question: "Is it possible to go through a whole day without spending any money on anything?"

For some people, it is best to work on a cash basis. (If you spend the actual dollar bills, instead of writing a check or charging, you will have a better feel for your money.)

Food
Food is a recurring expense. You'll be balancing the extra time needed to prepare cheaper meals against the money saved. Only you can set the balance.

The basic concept is to shop smarter. For example, when you pick up a can of pinto beans for sixty-five cents, you could buy that same handful of beans in bulk form for less than ten cents. True, you'd have to soak them overnight. But that takes only a moment to set up. The question is, would it be possible to do that with half the items on your shopping list? Following are some ideas that might help you think through food buying:

☐ Plan your menu around what is on sale.

☐ Never shop without a list, and buy *only* what is on your list.

☐ Try to buy as few things as possible that are not on sale.

☐ Choose a generic store brand over a national brand every time.

☐ Don't buy *any* prepared foods, such as frozen dinners or frozen vegetable mixtures.

☐ Never shop when you're hungry.

☐ Shop at discount clubs.

☐ Bake your own bread or buy day-old bread. Five day-old loaves of bread for a dollar will save a lot over the course of a month, if you're feeding several hungry kids.

☐ Buy whole chickens instead of cut-up parts.

☐ Involve your kids in the process of creatively planning meals. Ask them what they think the kids in Mexico, India or Africa might be eating. Then plan some of your meals to match what those kids eat. It will expose your family to another culture and connect you with your kids, plus save money.

☐ Learn to use beans, rice or potatoes—whatever is cheapest—to provide the mainstay for your meals. Instead of packaged cereal or Pop-tarts for breakfast, cook a cup of brown rice, add a few raisins or nuts that you bought in bulk and sprinkle on a little brown sugar. With or without milk, it's great, and you've fed three people for under a dollar.

☐ Look for the restaurants where kids eat free. Remember that in the midst of pain, it helps to have some special times.

It Isn't Fair!

No, it isn't fair. You have been forced to take on extra responsibility because of the abandonment, and yet you're supposed to do all this with less money. It is not fair!

You will always be balancing the competition between money and time. You can probably think of hundreds of ways to save money. But they all seem to cost you time—time you need to see lawyers, to reassure your kids, to find a better job, to adjust to being single, to spend some quiet time with God. Just take it one day at a time. Find your own balance of what works for you.

Financial reorganization is tough, but you will likely feel better as you get your money under *your* control. At least now you know it's going to your kids, not to an affair or to alcohol or some other addiction. Taking charge of your finances could be a very positive experience for you.

The abandoned woman has to be strong. Drastically cutting the budget is not easy to do. You'll find yourself repeatedly being angry at your husband for abandoning you. But the reality is that today you are abandoned—today you and your family must survive. When you make tough financial changes, you can be proud of yourself.

Keep focusing on God, who knows, cares and is involved in the thousands of details of your life. He is eager to help you. No, you're not going to be able to maintain your former lifestyle, but God is walking with you as you move to a new lifestyle.

The Lord loves those who hate evil; he protects the lives of his people, and rescues them from the wicked. Light is sown for the godly and joy for the good. (Ps 97:10-11)

—12—

Children

O*N A RECENT TELEVISION EPISODE OF* RESCUE 911, *WE SAW A* reenactment of two boys being electrocuted into unconsciousness. When their father rushed to the scene, he strenuously pulled one of the boys away from the electrical charge and quickly gave him mouth-to-mouth resuscitation. He then went back and with difficulty grabbed the second boy by his pants, pulled him away from the electrical charge and started trying to revive him as well.

As we watched that scene, the thought was running through our minds, *Which boy do you care for first? They are both your flesh and blood, and both are on the edge of dying if they don't get immediate help.* The father kept going back and forth between the two boys, giving them CPR until the 911 rescue team arrived.

After the team took the boys away in an ambulance, the father asked a reporter that very question: "How was I to decide which boy to help first?"

The story has a good outcome. Both boys lived, and both are working hard toward full recovery from the nearly fatal electrical shock.

The abandoned woman is in a similar situation. When her husband pulls away, suddenly she finds herself dealing with many desperate situations at the same time. Should she spend her time at the lawyer's office and at court, working through all of the legal maneuvering? Should she enter an intensive job-training program or go back to school to gain a new skill so that she can earn more money to support herself and the children?

Or should she spend time establishing new friends, going to divorce recovery groups and counseling sessions? Or should she do the extra maintenance work around the house? When does she have time for personal grooming or time to find a more economical car? The abandoned woman is now called upon to be Wonder Woman—an impossible role.

You might find help from a teeter-totter illustration. Remember when you were a kid playing with a friend in the schoolyard? You know how it was when one end of the teeter-totter was all the way down to the ground and the other person was stranded up in the air. If both people leaned toward the high end, the teeter-totter would start to move. Our reminder to Ann and to each person reading this book is: it isn't necessary to solve all of your problems at once. If you can make even a little movement in one area, you will notice an overall improvement in the other areas as well. You teeter-totter will be more balanced.

Helping Your Children Adjust

One of the major issues to face during this reconstruction period is how to help your children. The children need to continue to be kids, but they can also become allies with you in the process of reconstruction. Don't force them into adult roles or use them to replace adult friends, however. In truth, not only do you need to rebuild your life, but your children also must rebuild theirs. Following are several issues that might help you think through this task.

How much to tell the children. The abandoned woman typically goes to one of two extremes in communicating information to the children:

1. She doesn't tell the children anything, thinking that the less they know, the less they'll hurt.

2. She tells the children everything, especially how evil their father has been.

You need to find a middle ground. Consider the children's capacity to absorb information. If the children are very young, give them simple information in an easily understood form. On the other hand, older children can understand a lot more detailed information. Do *not* lie to them! Assure them that you'll always tell them the truth. Answer their questions, even if you don't share all the details.

It's also better to give truthful information on a regular basis right from the start, even daily, so the kids feel they are moving with the flow, and so they don't have to hear it from an outside source. At first you can tell the kids that you and Dad are having some trouble and that he has moved out to think a little. Make sure your information is not being given as a way to verify that their father is the bad guy and you are the good person. Remember that your husband is also the father of these children. They do have a connection to him that you should never try to destroy.

Assuming the roles of the father. In day-to-day life, you are now having to do many of your husband's jobs around the house. Even though you assume those roles, you must realize that your children will never view you as their father. They will always see you as their mother who has simply taken on some of Dad's jobs. You will never be able to help your sons become men in the same way your husband would have been able to do. In addition to his occasional input into their lives, they will need some outside male role models. Perhaps male relatives or friends can spend time helping with repairs in your home and teach your kids these skills. Or they can take the boys on outings for male bonding.

Visitation rights of the father. The divorce agreement ratified by the court will establish the visitation rights. They frequently are a deep source of annoyance for everyone involved. Someone is always late dropping the kids off or picking them up. Or there's a misunderstanding of the date or place they were going, or the kinds of clothes the kids were to wear. All of this may become a battleground for the former husband and wife to continue to beat on each other. Each of them seeks to prove that he or she is right and the other person is a rat. Tragically, the kids get caught in the crossfire and their self-image takes a battering.

Often parents notice that their kids are doing poorly in school, having trouble socially or carrying a great deal of anger. Each adult blames the other for the problems, rather than realizing that their fighting has created the children's problems.

Some parents and counselors feel that switching from one parent's home to the other can be damaging for children. Having to settle in at one place for a night, a weekend or longer, then pack and move to the other home, gives them a sense of instability.

When the relationship between the divorcing spouses is cordial, it may be possible to arrange that the children stay at the one parent's home every night, while they also have generous amounts of time with the other parent. For example, the dad might pick up the children early in the morning and have a wonderful outing with them until evening. Then they would still come home to their own beds and their own routine overnight. If the parents live nearby and are willing to do this for the sake of the children, it can help them live a more settled life.

Children's anger. Of course the children are angry! They're angry at their father and at their mother. They didn't ask for the divorce. Many children fully know that they *did not cause* the divorce; it was caused by their parents. Now why should they have to pay the price of all this pain and suffering because their parents goofed up?

Some children, however, believe very strongly that they did cause the divorce. They think to themselves, *If I had been a better kid, if I hadn't been so disobedient, if I hadn't caused fights in the house maybe they wouldn't be getting a divorce.* Whether children believe they are responsible or not, they experience great anger and sadness.

Unfortunately, your children may be angry not only at you and their father but also at God. They think, *Why did God allow this? I asked him to stop the divorce and to help my parents love each other, but he didn't. He must not care about us.*

Just as it's important to keep a regular flow of information going to your children, it's also important to keep draining off their anger. Open up the conversation with your children by using sentences such as these:

"You know, if I were a kid living through what you're going through, I would really be angry."

"I would feel that I'm getting gypped; I didn't cause the divorce, but my home is being broken up."

"I'd want to know: Why won't my parents listen to reason? Why don't they just forgive each other and love each other? It seems so simple. Why did they have to mess it all up for us?"

Putting yourself into the children's position helps them to see that you do understand some of their anger. It should help them open up and talk about it.

Another way to help them ventilate is to talk about other families that are breaking up. Ask them how those kids feel about their parents' divorce. "Which parent do you think is right or wrong in Mr. and Mrs. Jones's breakup? Do the kids take sides?"

Or ask them if they feel the church people did enough to help keep your marriage together or help your family through the divorce proceedings. Ask, "By the way, do you think God has been paying attention to what's been going on?" Find creative ways to help your children ventilate.

Remember to keep assuring your children that you didn't get divorced because they caused it or because you don't love them: "Your father and I love you very deeply. In fact, part of our fight is that we both want you to live with us because we both love you very much. Sometimes I'm so selfish that I don't want you to be with your father even for a weekend. I want you all to myself. But your father feels the same way."

Protecting your children. Sometimes when a family breaks up it is because a father is going through a mid-life crisis or some other crisis. He may begin to live a sharply different lifestyle from what he lived before. Previously, he may have been a church leader who was a straight and moral man. Suddenly his lifestyle may include drinking, hanging out at singles' bars or sleeping around—and no longer attending church.

A mother will find herself in a bind at this point. On the one hand, she wants to speak well of the father to the children and to fulfill her part of the divorce agreement for his visitation rights. But she doesn't want to expose the children to a very different moral standard than the one they have known thus far. So how does she cope?

Moreover, the mother may be so lonely that she looks to her children for emotional support, using them as intimate buddies. Tragically, she may use the children as adult substitutes, forcing them to unfairly bear her burdens.

The children must be protected. Each parent needs to be getting the help needed to make this transition through divorce.

Your lawyer is probably your best human ally to help you protect your children. An attorney can press for necessary modifications to visitation rights or child custody. The goal is not to punish the former husband but to protect the children.

Substitute fathers. A mother can never truly be a father to her children. She should encourage the children to relate to their father, and she also should introduce substitute fathers who can fill in where her husband doesn't.

When any separated or divorced father has regular time with the children, these times will be distorted from normal living because he is not with them on a day-to-day basis. He will always be playing catch-up in the few hours he is with them. He may be overly nice, playing the role of Santa Claus, or perhaps overly stern, trying to accomplish a lot of discipline in a few short hours. Unfortunately, even though a father tries to express commitment and love to the children, they will easily see that he has a divided allegiance, especially if and when he and his new wife have their first child.

Ann faced the realities connected with Bob's absence. Relatives could fill in some of the gaps. Couples within her small group were also willing to take on some parenting functions. She was glad for the church clubs that offered fun and adult role modeling to both Kim and Shawn.

Boyfriends as father substitutes? Some men that you date may try to parent your children. They may think they will earn points with you by acting like a father. Or if they are divorced men, they may seek to parent your children because they miss their own children.

The boyfriend as a substitute father will almost always fail. Remember, your children are still angry at you and your ex-husband. When you introduce a new man into the family setting, they are not likely to accept him right away. They still wish they could have their original family back.

Another reason children won't accept the new boyfriend as a father figure is that they're not sure you're actually going to marry this guy. Why should they make all kinds of emotional investments and become vulnerable to somebody who may be just your passing fancy?

On the other hand, it's not uncommon for children who are very needy to become strongly attached to the new boyfriend. If the relationship ends, the kids get hurt again.

It's better not to count on a boyfriend as being any help in parenting the children. It's more realistic for him to work at simply being a friend to your children. Look for role models and support groups through your local church or area clubs.

Bartering child care. Don't think of substitute parenting only as something other people do for you. Sometimes you can reciprocate. Take another couple's kids over a weekend, allowing the parents to get away to renew their marriage on a special retreat. Or offer your accounting skills to help a couple prepare their income tax in exchange for their taking your son on a weekend outing.

The point is that you don't want to think of yourself as a victim who must be cared for by other people. You are an independent woman, and you have a lot to offer to the world in general and to specific friends, as you all give to enrich each other's lives.

Helping Your Children Mature

You will be better able to help your kids if you remember that they will have different issues and questions than you do. They also will recover from the abandonment experience at a different pace than you will.

In order to help your children become adults, you need to focus on three basic areas of their lives. We refer to these as "the three *I*'s."

☐ Independence/Interdependence

☐ Identity
☐ Intimacy

Independence/interdependence. Notice that we are linking these two words together. You must make sure that your children do not become cripples because of this divorce. They must become independent people who can stand on their own feet. At the same time, they must be interdependent, meaning that they know how to link with other people. Your children should know how to serve and receive from other people, while still maintaining their own independence.

Identity. Your children must fully understand the special gifts God has given to them and how to use these gifts. Understanding who they are and that God has a special purpose for their lives will give them a sense of self-confidence and poise as they step into the world.

Intimacy. By intimacy we mean the giving and receiving of love. Frequently, people think of love as sex. But it is more accurate to think of love as giving yourself in order to enrich someone else. Your children should know how to give themselves in loving ways to build up other people. At the same time, they need to accept love from other people without conditions.

People who do not know how to give and receive love, who do not have a good sense of their identity and who don't understand their interdependence will have "boundary problems." They're not sure where their personhood stops and other people's starts. They may become easily manipulated, like puppets whose strings are controlled by someone else.

Now we come to an even more basic question. If we are supposed to produce within our children the three basic *I*'s, how do we do that? Many parents assume their kids will turn out okay if they just hang around with the family. Most of the time, kids do turn out okay if the parents are normally mature. The kids will automatically absorb some of the healthy traits and then be ready to face adult life. But in a family breakup they often absorb unhealthy ideas about marriage and relationships.

Intentionally raise your children so that they will become strong, mature adults who have recovered from the damage of the divorce. Here are three hints you can put into practice right now to build your children's confidence:

☐ Look into your children's eyes when you are relating to them. A full look into a person's eyes has a great deal of power. It convinces him or her of your sincerity. If you are looking elsewhere while you're talking, the child will not feel as important.

☐ Touch your children frequently. As you speak to them or pass them in a room, reach out and touch them on the hand or shoulder, or put your arm around them. Human touch is a powerful bonding factor. If children are only told that they are loved, they are not as likely to believe it as if they are also hugged. Reach out and pat your kids or give them a squeeze whenever you come near them. (With adolescents you may get some resistance at first! But they may secretly love it.) If you haven't done much of this in the past, start slowly and develop the habit.

☐ Talk to them frequently. Show an interest in what is going on in their lives. Keep conversation flowing as freely as possible. And don't make your kids guess whether you love them. Look squarely into their faces, reach out and touch them, and then use words to say, "I really love you; I'm glad you're part of this family. I'm sorry we're going through this stress right now, but I want you to know that I love you."[1]

As you combine all of these actions, you'll be playing a very powerful part in helping your children to recover from the abandonment and to grow in maturity.

Powerful Tools for Parenting

Following are some strong principles to help you as you continue with the parenting process.

1. Teach. The Bible gives you the responsibility as a parent of teaching your children. Sometimes the abandoned woman feels she has lost her right to teach her children because her marriage has broken up or that in her present confusion about life she has nothing to offer them. But a broken marriage doesn't change the Bible's charge to you: "Teach a child to use the right path, and when he is older he will remain upon it" (Prov 22:6). And you have a *lot* to offer them.

The idea of teaching implies whetting the appetite. Your teaching or training should come in a positive way that will stimulate your children to learn biblical values and grow—not from coercion but from modeling and timely insights.

Your role is to be a coach, not a dictator. Think of yourself as a friend, helping your children become all they can be. Being a friend doesn't mean that you become childish, but that you understand their struggles.

The promise in that Proverbs 22 verse is conditional. Teaching your children to use the right path means that you must help them discover the unique gifting and ability God has given to each child—and encourage that development. Then, when your children become mature, they will not forsake the moral values and training you have helped them discover.

Sometimes parents force children into a certain activity, such as music or sports, instead of helping them try many different directions to see where God has gifted them. These children may see the parents' moral teachings as another forced feeding—to be rejected. Think again of "whetting" and "stimulating." Help your children discover moral values for themselves. Then those will be their values, not just yours. Talking over questions and bringing up sticky issues of life will help your children to mature in God's pattern.

2. Offer love and acceptance. Love and acceptance are two sides of one coin. On the one hand, you accept your kids where they are right now in their development. You also accept the reality that they will regress several times during the ups and downs of recovery after the abandonment. On the other hand, you see where they need to be moving, and you try to guide them in the right direction. Love and acceptance do not mean you roll over and play dead as a parent; love includes guidance, and love sometimes has to be tough.

Giving in to your children is very easy for the abandoned woman. You may lose perspective because you feel unworthy. *I'm not a good mate, so how can I train my children? I'll compensate for my failure by loving and indulging them as a "sugar mama" instead of loving and guiding them by saying no.* In order for them to mature, you must say no sometimes and point the direction. Firmness may seem painful at this time, but it's the needed ingredient for growth and maturity.

Your children will be better able to handle the hard growth they must go through if you continue to look them in the face as you talk to them, touch and hug them, and tell them how much you love them. Let them know that you want only God's very best for their lives.

3. Set boundaries. Children need to know that they are distinct persons who are separate from you and that they have their own identities. Children in a single-parent home frequently have their boundaries violated. The single parent often unconsciously tries to push the children into the role of the missing parent by forcing extra work on them or by forcing them to become a counselor, buddy and companion to the lonely single parent.

Say directly to your children, "We need to talk about boundaries. We are a family. We are all experiencing this divorce situation together, but each of us is an individual too. It's important to respect the privacy and the possessions of each person in this family. A lot of changes are going on now, and each of us is going to have to take on more responsibility. It's important that

172

we talk to each other about this and not cross over each other's boundaries." Make a list together, including such rules as these: Each person can have a private place to keep treasures. Everybody should knock before entering another's bedroom. The kids don't have to tell Mom any more than they want to about their visit at Dad's place.

Parents need to be parents; children need to be children. Avoid the temptation to cross your children's boundaries by making them your confidants. Don't talk to your children in great detail about *all* of your feelings. Acknowledge that you are all going through a hard time, but remind them that God is pulling for each of you.

When your children prepare to visit their father, talk with them about the boundaries issue: "Be yourself. Be the special person whom God has created you to be. You don't have to do things that you don't agree with just because a friend, or even your father, says you should. If it is morally wrong, don't do it. Just tell the person, 'I don't feel good about doing this; I'd rather not do it.' "

4. Give your kids priority time. Children need to know that they are high on your schedule. Don't think so much in terms of hours and minutes, but of being with them in a focused way. Work on looking at them, touching and talking to them. Ten minutes of your full attention will mean more than an hour of being together while you are half-focused on something else.

In the abandonment situation, everything needs your attention at once. It will be easy not to spend time with your kids, especially if they are rather compliant. However, sometimes kids will become obnoxious and difficult to live with as a way to get your attention and force you to spend time with them.

Remember, you *will* spend time with your kids, either because you choose to or because they force you to. They may unconsciously disrupt the family or get in trouble with the law or in their date life. Keep verbally affirming them, looking into their face and giving them hugs. They have experienced a great loss in this family, and they may not have the support network you have.

5. Be a consistent model. How will your kids become wonderful, mature, responsible adults with positive self-images, making a good impact on the world? Much will be absorbed from you as they watch the way you handle this situation with all of its explosive elements.

We hope that your children will see you trusting God and quietly putting the pieces of your life back together again. They need to see all facets of your personality—when you are discouraged as well as when you're "up" and feeling successful. Let them see some of your mood changes appropriate to their ages. Talk with them about your sadness—then also live out before them your deep confidence in God, your awareness of who you are and what you have to offer to the world.

They need to see you standing strong in the face of abandonment and abuse. They also need to see you as a gentle person who can forgive, be tender and reach out to help other people. Your children will probably catch more from you by spiritual osmosis than they will absorb through your direct teaching.

6. Internalize values. Your children must not go through their teen years and into adulthood accepting only your values. The choices they make in life must rest on their own internal values. Your teenagers should never say, "I don't drink because my mother thinks drinking is wrong." Rather, they should say, "I don't drink because it's wrong for me." They should wrestle through these questions long before they are confronted with them so they will have strong convictions upon which to make their choices when the time comes.

To help this happen, share your life with your children. Talk with them about why you make the choices you do. Don't just say, "Do it because I say so." Give them ten reasons why you don't do something. Let them in on your reasoning, your thought process. Deliberately raise questions: "What do you think about my reasons for not drinking? How would you feel if I told you that I didn't think we should lie, and then you caught me telling a lie?" Help your children wrestle with moral values. Don't hush them up; don't try to get them to think the way you think. Their values must come from deep within themselves.

Another way to help children develop their own values is to share your caring for people with your children. If you take food to a sick friend, let the children help you prepare the food or carry it in to your friend. If you chat awhile with your friend, include your children—and give them a chance to talk. A five-year-old's wandering tale about kindergarten may delight your friend as well as build your child's confidence and enjoyment.

Ask one of the kids to pray for your sick friend. Whatever you do in caring for other people, involve the children so they'll understand that they are interconnected with other people and are not simply islands in the sea by themselves or pitiful victims of abandonment.

7. *Let your children care for you.* We are not suggesting that you suddenly become dependent, with your children meeting your needs. Rather, understand that it's good for your kids to express their love for you and to do things for you. It's necessary for them to learn to serve. They need to see the family as a mutual support network, not an organization where the leadership and support come only from the top down.

A good way to reinforce children in helping you is for you to tell them how much you appreciate them anytime they care for you. For example, if one of them is leading in prayer at the dinner table and asks God to help you through this tough time, then immediately after the prayer, look the child in the eye, touch him or her and say, "I want you to know how deeply that touched me to know that you care for me that way. Thank you very much."

When kids do something a bit sacrificial or unusually helpful, such as keeping their room slightly neater, hauling out the trash without being nagged or helping to clear the table without being asked, affirm them verbally and with a touch. Watch for those special voluntary times when they show a helpful spirit, and then give strong affirmation. People tend to repeat anything for which they are praised. Your praising may start a whole new direction in the character and maturing of your children.

8. *Remind yourself and the kids that God cares.* Many times you will feel that you are in this battle by yourself. You will feel alone, not only because your former husband has left you with the responsibility of raising the children, but also because he has actually made it harder. He has caused confusion in the children's minds about marriage and other life values.

The abandonment has dumped what seem to be ten thousand problems on you to handle—all at the same time. But take hope and keep on reflecting on one of our favorite verses: "For I know the plans I have for you, says the Lord. They are plans for good and not for evil, to give you a future and a hope. In those days when you pray, I will listen. You will find me when you seek me, if you look for me in earnest" (Jer 29:11-13).

Continually remind yourself that God not only knows about what is happening but is also deeply concerned—*for you.* Ask him for the wisdom and insights that you need. Ask him to help you say the right words during those teachable moments when your kids are pliable. Ask him to give you strength and sensitivity to speak each time your kids experience a positive accomplishment. Keep on expecting God to work in your life and in your children's lives.

Let God also speak to you through your friends. Tell your

friends you need to hear their encouragement about how you are doing. It will help a lot to hear, "Ann, you're doing great with the kids," or "We're proud of the way you're handling all the stress you're going through. You are becoming an even better person in this tough time."

It might be helpful to start keeping a prayer notebook. On one half of the page, jot down the things that you are praying for. Make your requests very small and very specific. (It's okay to be praying for the big things, but it's difficult to tell when you get answers.) When you get an answer, put it on the page next to the request. It will encourage you, when you wonder if prayer is being answered, to look at a few pages and see that God, in fact, is answering prayer, and his plans for you are "for good and not for evil."

O God, you have helped me from my earliest childhood—and I have constantly testified to others of the wonderful things you do. And now that I am old and gray, don't forsake me. Give me time to tell this new generation (and their children too) about all your mighty miracles. (Ps 71:17-18)

—13—

Selfhood

*A*NN CALLED US ON THE PHONE. SHE WAS TRYING TO BE COMPOSED, but she started to cry angrily as she explained that she had bumped into Bob and Jennifer downtown They hadn't seen her, but she had just about gone wild at seeing the two of them together.

They had pulled up in front of the travel agency in Bob's sporty new four-wheel-drive Bronco. Bob got out; then Jennifer slid out the driver's side. Ann assumed that Jennifer had been snuggling next to Bob. The sight of Jennifer in her short shorts made Ann boil with anger. *How could Bob be so stupid as to let Jennifer break up our marriage?* she thought. Then they put their arms around each other and walked into the travel agency.

Ann somehow managed to go about her business, but her heart was pounding and she almost forgot where she was. She was seething with anger all over again at this whole sordid process. She tried to do her shopping without thinking about Bob and Jennifer, but she couldn't get the scene out of her mind.

Finally she finished her errands and walked back to her car. She noticed the Bronco was gone. She had a friend at the travel agency. On the spur of the moment, she ignored her better judgment and went in to see her friend and to ask what Bob and Jennifer were planning. Part of her said she shouldn't be spying on them, but her anger and jealousy pushed her through the door.

Maria, who owned the travel agency, was Ann's good friend. She had arranged many of Bob and Ann's trips, as well as all of Bob's "business trips." Maria was very angry at Bob for abandoning Ann, so automatically she was on Ann's side. She felt no need to withhold any information about where Bob and Jennifer were going on vacation.

Maria pulled out a map of the Pacific and said, "First they're flying to Hawaii for a week, visiting four of the islands. And you know Bob, he always wants to be in the very best hotels. Even after they've been married for months, he's still trying to show off for Jennifer.

"Then they're flying to Fiji for four days—and then they'll spend twelve days on the Tahitian islands. I think it's all wrong, Ann. That should be *you* going with Bob. This divorce just isn't right."

Ann told us that deep within she knew this information was not helping her; it only made her more angry and jealous. But she also felt good about Maria's affirmation. She felt vindicated every time someone took her side. After Ann dumped all this information on us over the phone, she asked if she could see us soon.

When she sat down in the office the next day, she was under better control. The trip incident was an opportunity for her to work on reconstructing her self-image. She had been severely damaged psychologically by the abandonment, and now it was necessary to take action to deliberately rebuild her sense of self. She must not allow herself to drift or to be manipulated by events in Bob and Jennifer's life.

Facing his abandonment—"take two." For many months you will replay the abandonment. It will sweep over you again and again. Each time, think about the issues you have worked through and the positive results. Replaying those will help you to become a stronger person. Remember especially these items:

☐ Grieving you have done
☐ The "grace forgiveness"
☐ Burning the slips of pain
☐ Symbolic burial

Keep on focusing on *what is,* not on what you imagine. The trip incident gave Ann a good opportunity to confirm *what is* to herself—*I'm not going with Bob on this trip; Jennifer is. I'm divorced.* Don't allow your mind to click back into what *should be.* And don't allow it to click back into blame.

Ann had released Bob into God's hands; yet when new incidents happened she had to repeat the process. Anytime the pressure starts to build for you, let loose and commit it all into God's hands. Every time you bravely face the abandonment, you are strengthening your self-image.

Assertiveness. As Ann faced Bob's abandonment, we saw a very positive, strong Ann come through with a great deal of assertiveness. She handled that whole process of getting friends together, the forgiveness and the mock burial very, very well. Each time she was assertive, her sense of self improved. She felt more in control and like a worthwhile person. She had setbacks, but each time she moved ahead a little farther.

Change is gradual. We remind you that you shouldn't beat up on yourself. You are not God. You are an imperfect being, as are the rest of us. All of us are trying to figure out life. So be good to yourself; realize that your change to a stronger self is a gradual one that will take time.

Telling other people. We said to Ann, "Do you remember how good it felt when you found out that Maria knew about Bob and Jennifer? Telling other people about Bob's abandonment is going to help your self-image to be stronger."

Tell your story honestly. Share not only the fact that your husband abandoned you but also what you are learning about your part in the failure of the marriage and how you are growing. Giving people accurate information will help them have a deeper respect for you. They'll see you as a person in control, not a victim, and you will feel their affirmation. So tell your close friends, the people at church, your friends in your various groups and the people at work.

A good way to plan for sharing this information with people is to draw several concentric circles. Then list the people in the various circles, starting with the center circle—people closest to you. The ones in the inner circle should know first and know the most details; then keep on moving out to the more peripheral people. Your self-image will grow through each experience of telling, even if some people disapprove, withdraw or imply blame.

Physical recovery. You've got to see your whole person as interconnected—including your body. Not only has your psychological self-image taken a beating, but so have your physical reserves and your immune system. As you work on improving your self-image, you'll notice your physical body and immune system will start to recover.

The opposite is also true. As you help your physical body to recover, your self-image will be positively affected. Following are some things to use as checkpoints to help your body recover:

Exercise. If possible, try to get at least twenty to thirty minutes of good exercise every day. Exercise changes the chemical makeup of your brain, enabling you to handle stress more easily and giving you a greater sense of well-being. Keep varying your exercise program so that your body has a better tone to it. Get your muscles in shape. You may weigh the same, but you'll see the flab go away and be replaced by muscle. As your toning improves, you'll feel better about yourself as well as being physically healthier.

Food. Focus on eating good foods, not on losing weight. Minimize the use of fats, sugar, caffeine and alcohol. Build your diet around fresh fruits and vegetables and complex carbohydrates (breads, potatoes, rice, pasta, cereals). You don't have to eliminate meat and fish, but use those as a garnish rather than as the main part of your meal.

Sleep. You've learned very important lessons about releasing anxiety and your husband to God. Those releasing techniques will help you sleep better. Your body needs to recover, so get at least eight hours of sleep a night. If it's hard to get to sleep, try a warm bath or a glass of warm milk at bedtime. One woman shared with us that she fell asleep each night with her stereo playing soft, relaxing hymns of assurance and hope. Bedtime is a good time to talk with God, turning over to him all of the day's anxieties, asking his care upon you and your family for the nighttime hours and all the days ahead.

Don't be embarrassed if you sleep longer some days or take a nap on the weekend. Listen to your body and remember that its healing is closely related to your positive self-image.

New self-reliance skills. Everything has been dumped in your lap, including all the household and yard stuff your husband used to do. Remember, he was not some sort of world-class genius. He just had picked up a few maintenance skills throughout his life—and so can you.

It's no big deal to change a light bulb; likewise, you can learn to change a tire or coach a high-school son on how to trim bushes and mow the lawn. Every time you learn a skill related to house or car maintenance—something that you thought was your husband's domain—you'll find yourself appreciating who you are and what you can do. So take the risk! Plunge in! Most of the skills for maintaining a house and car can be learned by reading a good home-repair book and practicing. Go for it.

Another trick is to barter skills. If someone wants a recipe for your special bread, say, "It's more than just a recipe—it's learning how to do it. I'll show you how to bake it if you'll bring your husband along and have him show me how to change a tire and what to check for under the hood." Bartering skills will make you feel good about yourself in two ways: you're teaching your friend an important skill, and you're learning a skill you need.

Go with your heart interests. You've been putting off taking a painting class or pursuing some other hobby. The community college and other groups offer classes for various interests. Why not go with your heart? Find a course that fits your schedule and take it. Perhaps you used to play a lot of tennis; maybe that would be a good way to get exercise and rekindle an old pastime. Or you may find a class in the American novel or doll-making or swimnastics.

Modify your life pattern to fit your interests, and your self-image will become more positive. God has made you a special person. Respond to that uniqueness in as many ways as you can. Then you'll be living your life, not out of *ought to's,* but as a match with God's gifting.

Compensation. Turn this bad thing called abandonment into positive insights and help for other people. I (Jim) like to sail. Even though the wind is blowing across a lake in one direction, I can adjust the sail and rudder to go anywhere I want on the lake. It's not the wind that dictates my direction; it's what I do with the wind. The same is true with abandonment. You can adjust your emotional sails to use this desertion as a positive factor in your life and to help other people.

Start looking for other abandoned women. Maybe it's time to form a small group and help others work through the same things you've worked through. Ask your church education director if he or she could suggest a spiritually mature woman who has survived abandonment and could lead a group. Or perhaps you could teach a class on divorce prevention or recovery.

As you deliberately compensate and allow God to turn evil into good, you will like yourself more. Being a growing, contributing person not only helps other people with their problems, but also helps you to feel better about your life.

Let people help you. When people offer to help you, accept their offers. But be careful not to exploit them. That's why thinking in terms of bartering skills and time is a good plan: it's a way to give help as well as to get help for yourself.

Lots of groups offer help. A church in our community has a group for women whose husbands are involved in affairs. Many church and community organizations have divorce-recovery groups. Take advantage of the insights and support that these groups and your helping friends can give.

Not a victim. Allowing other people to help you can either reinforce the victim mentality or lift you above the problem. Continue to reach out to encourage other people. As you help them with their problems, you will move away from a "poor me" attitude.

Here are some tips that may help guarantee that you won't get trapped in the victim mentality:

Think positive thoughts. The Bible says, "Fix your thoughts on what is true and good and right. Think about things that are pure and lovely, and dwell on the fine, good things in others. Think about all you can praise God for and be glad about" (Phil 4:8).

Question yourself. Each time you find yourself feeling sorry for yourself or nursing that victim mentality, ask yourself, *How long am I going to stay angry at my husband? How long am I going to be his victim, manipulated by his betrayal? Will I keep this up for six months? Is that enough time? How about a year, two years, five years?*

It's time to finally say, *Enough is enough! I'm not going to be a victim!* Remember the Bible can help you refocus your thought life.

Ask your friends to keep you accountable. Tell them that you're trying to break out of feeling that you are a victim. Ask them to speak a gentle word to you each time they see you falling prey to that attitude of feeling sorry for yourself.

Seek counseling. Speak frankly to your counselor about your victim feelings. Ask the counselor to help you not be controlled by your husband's betrayal.

Focus on God. He is your ally and he wants to help you through this time. He wants you to become more than you ever thought you could be. We frequently pray this scriptural prayer with people:

I have never stopped thanking God for you. I pray for you constantly, asking God, the glorious Father of our Lord Jesus Christ, to give you wisdom to see clearly and really understand who Christ is and all that he has done for you. I pray that your hearts will be flooded with light so that you can see something of the future he has called you to share. I want you to realize that God has been made rich because we who are Christ's have been given to him! I pray that you will begin to understand how incredibly great his power is to help those who believe in him. It is that same mighty power that raised Christ from the dead and seated him in the place of honor at God's right hand in heaven. (Eph 1:16-20)

The Life-Changing Dream
Ann worked intermittently on reconstructing her self-image.

Then she shared with us a dream she had—a dream that gave her a new sense of hope and a positive perspective.

She said, "You know how dreams are sort of stories that don't really fit with the way your life is, but you clearly understand the message the dream is trying to tell you? Well, that's the kind of dream I had last night.

"I was a little girl, and I was playing with my friend, but I was not at my own house. So I started walking home. I was out in the country—like one of those roads on *The Waltons*. I was walking down this country lane all by myself, and I was barefoot, wearing an old dress.

"I walked toward the sunset, but the evening kept getting darker and darker. Finally, as it was almost dark, I realized that I was lost. I knew I was going toward home, but I didn't know where it was, and I didn't know how to go back to my friend's home.

"Suddenly I saw the beam of a flashlight coming out of the woods beside the road. A kind-looking man said to me, 'Hi, little girl, are you lost?'

"I said, 'Yes,' and he said, 'Let me help you.' I wasn't the least bit afraid of him. In fact, I felt as if he were an old friend I'd known for a long time. I felt safe with him, but I didn't recognize his face.

"He held my hand as we walked down the lane, his flashlight beam lighting the road ahead of us. I felt very secure because I seemed to know him—he was so easy to talk to. I don't know what we talked about, but it seemed as if we talked about everything.

"Then the lane opened onto a clearing. On the one side was a large house with all the lights on. Many people were inside, and I could hear laughing, singing and lots of talking. The people obviously were happy and having a good time.

"As we walked up the driveway to the house, I felt as if I

belonged in this house—as if this were my home. But it was not my parents' home; it was my adult home. As we got closer to the house, I could see through the window. The people inside were all my friends. They seemed to be expecting me.

"I let go of the stranger's hand and started to walk to the door. Just before I got to the door, I realized I was no longer a little girl, but a grown woman. I turned to thank the stranger. As I saw his face, he was not a stranger; I realized it was God himself.

"I said, 'Thank you very much for helping me find my way home.'

"He responded, 'If you ever get lost again, I'll always be near.' "

Ann continued, "I turned and walked into the house to be with my friends, knowing that God was also in the house with me and my friends. I also knew that he would be outside the door if I should ever get lost again.

"You know," she said, "I've had a deep settled peace since that dream. I know life isn't going to be easy. I have lots of hard things to work through. But I know that God is always with me, whether I'm inside the house having fun with my friends, or outside the house—and lost."

I waited patiently for God to help me; then he listened and heard my cry. He lifted me out of the pit of despair, out from the bog and the mire, and set my feet on a hard, firm path and steadied me as I walked along. He has given me a new song to sing, of praises to our God. (Ps 40:1-3)

—14—

Dating
and Sex

*A*BOUT SEVEN MONTHS AFTER HER DIVORCE FROM BOB WAS FINAL, Ann sat in our office and shared an incident that had deeply unsettled her. She'd had lunch with an old male friend, and suddenly her world was in turmoil. She thought she had life pretty well organized and everything was finally under control. But then Philip appeared. "It seems as if I've lost my way again," she said.

She went on to explain, "It was only a few weeks after Bob left that the word started to get around. Frankly, I was shocked by the men who started to hit on me. They were everywhere: at work, at church, where I shopped for groceries or clothes, even where I had my car fixed.

"I'm a thirty-eight-year-old woman. I have two children. I'm not some kind of supermodel. So I was just blown away over and over again as I became aware that men were watching me.

In fact, I've been too embarrassed to talk about it, even to the two of you, until now.

"You see, when Bob abandoned me, I felt like dirt. I felt I had failed in marriage and was a totally undesirable person. If Bob didn't want me, certainly no one else would. That's why I was so surprised to find men looking at me as if they were interested in me.

"I found myself wrestling with two different emotions. On the one hand, because I was totally disgusted with and angry at Bob, I wanted nothing to do with men at all. I had felt that Bob was a man I could trust, but then he betrayed me. So now all of those feelings from my childhood and high school came to the surface again. I've been struggling with an absolute distrust of all men.

"In fact, Jim, that's one of the things I've had to wrestle with in our counseling sessions. It's good that I've been able to talk to the two of you together, because Sally's presence has helped me to trust you. I probably wouldn't have trusted you if she were not a joint counselor with you.

"The other interesting fact about the attention I've gotten from men is that part of me really liked it. I had made a decision that I was going to have nothing to do with men, I would never remarry, and I probably would never date. Yet I've found that a man's appropriate remark such as 'You are a fun and intelligent person to work with' feels good. Of course, I've been totally turned off by those jerks who sexually harass me and make me feel as if they only see my body.

"The point is, *I don't need a man*. Before I tell you about what happened with my old friend Phil, I want you to know how well I've been doing. I'm in a small group, and I'm expanding my circle of women who are close companions. That has worked very well. I'm really a very happy person. I have not found singleness to be a problem. I can honestly say that I don't need a man to lean on.

"I'm not saying that I don't want men involved in my life, but during these months I've learned that I don't need a husband or boyfriend. In fact, I've been able to develop 'brother-sister' relationships with men that are a lot deeper than when I was married.

"I've learned the difference between living alone and being lonely. Just because I live alone, without a husband, that doesn't mean I need to be lonely. Several of my married women friends are very much lonelier—their marriage relationships are really sour. So a husband doesn't necessarily solve the loneliness factor in a woman's life. Being lonely is my own personal problem. It's an issue between myself and God. Sometimes I can be in a room full of my friends and yet feel very lonely.

"One of the things that has helped me in the loneliness problem is deepening my relationship with God. I turned that corner when God gave me the dream of his meeting me on that dark country road and taking me home. I came to realize that if I have a strong connection with God, I will never really be lonely—whether I am married or not. Once I disconnected living alone from being lonely, it simply became a matter of learning to cope with the new responsibilities.

"I also learned to transfer some of my companionship needs away from Bob to the women in my small circle of friends, as well as to people in my other groups. In fact, as I've gotten more involved with other people, I've begun to realize that Bob and I had lost a lot of our companionship. We were just running the business of marriage and family but were not companions.

"I was also grateful for your warning to watch out that I didn't transfer my companionship needs to my children. I wanted them to have their own lives, but at times I was tempted to turn them into my companions instead of just being a mother to them.

"Frankly, the worst part of this whole process was handling my friends and relatives. I'm sure they were well meaning, but they were pests. Always trying to fix me up. You know, I think a lot of people feel you're weird if you're not married. Some of my relatives and friends are like that. I'm glad I had settled some of the other issues in my life so that I could say very directly, 'No, I don't want to date. I am a whole person without a man ' "

A New Adventure

"But Philip is different. All of this is leading up to the really important thing that I want to talk about. Suddenly all of my organized, controlled life is coming unglued. I've got these funny feelings. I had satisfied myself and put off my friends by saying, 'I don't need a man.' Suddenly Philip appeared from out of my past, and I feel as if I'm being pulled in two different directions.

"It reminds me of the first time I went parasailing." (That's where a speedboat has a long rope attached to it, a parachute is attached to the rope and a rider is strapped into the parachute.) "I was on the beach and the motorboat was out about three hundred yards. I was told to run toward the water as the boat started to move. Then, as I ran along, the parachute would fill with air and lift me off the ground. I very much wanted to go parasailing and feel the exhilaration of floating above the coastline. At the same time, I had been having a good time relaxing on the sandy beach. But I couldn't stay on the beach if I went parasailing. And I did enjoy the adventure of parasailing!"

Ann summarized, "That's the way it is with Philip. It seems as if he wants to take me on an emotional parasailing ride, yet I'm very comfortable the way I am.

"Part of me feels like a sixteen-year-old who is being asked to go on her first special date. But the other part of me is a cynical woman who has been burned over and over again by men. I'm contented with my life as it is. I don't want to risk the possibility of harm. So—I realize that I'm at a tension point in my life. But I've come through a divorce; I can solve this too."

The basics. We told Ann we wanted her to know that we were very proud of her. She had done a lot of growing and changing. She was more stable now than we had ever known her to be. Even though Bob's abandonment had caused her terrible pain, it had become a positive strength, producing mature and caring qualities in her.

You as the reader need to think about several factors if an appealing man walks into your life. You've invited God into your life. In fact, you've asked him to direct it. So it may be that God is now moving you to a different phase of your experience.

If you have found many men being attracted to you or even "hitting on you," you may not have felt the need to respond to them. In fact, the more that men expressed an interest in you, the more you may have been turned off.

But suddenly a certain man walks into your life and you just about flip out. Could this be God working to prepare you for the next season of life?

Don't jump too quickly. That man might be like Ann's parasailing experience. He seems to be sweeping you right off the beach into the ecstasy of flight. But ask yourself, *Is he sent to be my companion? Or is he sent by God to simply open my life up to other male companionships?*

God knows you need a man you can trust to make you tender again toward men. Don't jump to the conclusion that because this guy is sweeping you off your feet, you should marry him. Remember to be cautious. You need time to:

☐ discover what went wrong in your first marriage

☐ make changes and grow

☐ know God better

☐ stabilize your personal and family life

Old fears reappear. As you allow a man to care for you, it's going to remind you again of your husband's abandonment. Also, the old wounds from your childhood and young adulthood are going to reappear. You'll find yourself suspecting the motives of the men you date, wondering if they can be trusted or if they too will abandon you.

Part of the reason you've been telling yourself that you don't need a man is that it's an easy way to avoid some of your hurtful issues. Just thinking about dating will open up your mind to those problems. That's not necessarily bad. This may be a good time to settle those issues a bit more. However, you shouldn't get into a serious relationship with any man until those fears are put to rest.

We're not telling you not to date. In fact, dating may help you face those issues that you've been trying to avoid or that have been only partially dealt with. God may feel it's time for another growth spurt in your life. Perhaps he's going to use men to help you face some of those old wounds. Remember that God said to Ann in her dream, "Whenever you get lost, I'm right here." Keep that in mind as you go through this next phase.

If you take things slowly, you won't be overcome by the risk of being vulnerable to men. Settle your mind to take it slowly. Communicate your fears honestly with any man you date. Then you'll reduce your sense of anxiety. If God is in the relationship, you don't have to worry that honesty will drive him away.

A good way to take it slowly is to let a man know that you want to date in groups, or at least double date. If he seems pushy, let him know that you are not ready to date only one man.

You have an active social life of church, bowling, dinners, visiting museums, picnics at the beach. Perhaps now is the time to invite a man to join you and the group. Make it clear to him that it's not a date. You want to be with the whole group and continue to enjoy all the men and women in the group. Group dating is safe, yet it will still force you to face your life issues connected to abandonment.

When you get more comfortable with group dating, you might

want to start double or triple dating. There's safety in numbers, and double or triple dating implies less commitment than a date alone.

Keep reminding yourself, *If God is in this process, I don't have to worry about losing one man if I date other men.* The right man will still be there; don't let time worry you.

The question always comes up, "When do I know that I've dated enough? Am I ready to date just one man and eventually go through an engagement period?" The answer to that is very simple. When you've worked through your unresolved issues and the fear in you subsides, you're ready. When you can look at all the pieces of your life objectively and the most logical next step is to spend more time with just one man—you're ready.

If your circumstances and preferences lead you to proceed with your life without finding another husband, don't feel that that is abnormal or unhealthy. We are not implying that every woman needs marriage.

Cautions about the dating game. Most people date with their emotions and not much rational thinking. Before you get too deep in any relationship, think about the dating process. Your maturity and experience will make dating easier than when you started dating in your teen years.

Over the next several days, specifically think about the following areas:

1. What do I want in a man? Make a list of the traits you want in a man. Don't let your anger at abandonment cause you automatically to cross off your ex-husband's strong traits from your list. You've seen a lot of life, a lot of marriages and you've known a lot of people. All of that should enable you to list at least twelve top traits.

2. Who am I and what do I bring to a relationship? Imagine that you're talking on the phone to someone across the country whom you've never met and you're explaining to him who you are. Your list should include all that you've been learning about yourself. Your rebuilt self-image will help you make this list.

3. Avoid exploitive men. I (Sally) grew up on a farm where we raised many different crops, plus we had a big garden, a dairy herd, pigs, sheep and chickens. Chickens have a very cruel nature. When a chicken becomes sick, the other chickens start pecking it until they've pecked it to death.

Exploitive men are like that, especially if you act as if you are a victim of abandonment. They sense it and want to take advantage of you. In fact, exploitive men will *seem* to be the most caring men. They hope they can manipulate you into bed if they act as if they really care for you. So don't behave like a victim. Believe that God is caring for you—you don't have to put up with exploitive men.

4. Set boundaries. In *Sexual Harassment No More,* three chapters talk about how a woman can reduce sexual harassment. In a section entitled "Don't Fan the Flames," we caution:

Yes, men must take responsibility—but women should not unnecessarily light fires. You can avoid some sexual harassment by knowing that men are turned on differently than women. Men are very visual and have short fuses. Watch the way you dress.

Let's get specific. Don't go braless. Don't wear tight-fitting clothes. If you have a choice, wear a longer rather than a shorter skirt. And don't wear clothes that people can see through or low necklines that men can look down into when you lean over.

Don't talk about sex scenes in movies or tell sexually oriented jokes. It's wrong for men and it's wrong for women. Sometimes women try to show they are equal by talking as dirty as men. This approach only demeans a woman and plays into men's hands.

Sensual comments and actions lead men on. Remember

they are already oversexualizing all you say and do. Don't perch on the edge of a man's desk with your legs crossed. He thinks you're asking him to respond.[1]

Learn to say no when your boundaries are violated. Listen to your inner heart. If you feel uncomfortable with a man, his words or his actions, then get away from him.

5. *You may have to change churches or groups.* For example, sometimes a divorce-recovery group may spend too much time focusing on the past, which keeps you from moving on to a new segment of your life. If the church you are attending is very judgmental, with a restrictive view of divorce and remarriage, you may be forced to find another place of fellowship. (People hold very different views on the biblical texts about divorce and remarriage. Go to a Christian bookstore to find some books as resources.)

6. *What and when do you tell his/your children?* Dating puts you and your children in a delicate position. You don't want your kids becoming emotionally attached to every man you date. Nor do you want the opposite extreme that a college student shared with us, "I had never met the man until the day of the wedding—at the front of the church, where I gave my mother to him."

Remember your promise to the children. Be honest and answer all their questions. Let them know you have several men friends. Give your kids information about your new friends as you would if they were women friends. This is also a time to help your kids work through any anger from the divorce—your dating may bring it to the surface again. When you start to date one man exclusively, let the kids know that. The children's emotional attachment to any man should be a few levels behind yours.

However, when the two of you decide to get married, take your time about announcing it to the kids. Work first at helping them come to a comfortable acceptance of the possibility of your future marriage. Your engagement announcement and marriage plans should not catch your children or your friends uncomfortably off-guard.

Let's Talk About Sex

It's better that we talk about sex than pretend it's not going to be a problem. The difficulty is that you've been married for a long time and have probably had sex frequently. When you find yourself comfortably attracted to a man, you may find it difficult not to continue the pattern of frequent sex that you had with your former husband. And because you've been married a long time, you've forgotten how to say, "No!"

When you were a teenager you probably had clearly established stopping points, because of your parental training and religious convictions. When you were on a date, you became nervous if a boy started to move his hands close to your breasts. If he kept going, you would finally tell him, "Stop!"

But after you were married for a while, you became accustomed to your husband slipping his arms around you while you were preparing the evening meal. You wouldn't stop him as he kissed you on the neck and gently touched your body. The only thing that would stop you from going to bed immediately was that the kids were waiting for dinner.

Now it's different. You may find yourself dating men who also don't have any stop lines. They also may have been accustomed to frequent sex in marriage. Sex has been a natural flow for both of you over these past years. Now you must clearly set your boundaries for new relationships.

The more intimate you are with a person, the more you will be emotionally bonded to that person. If the two of you honestly share your fears and joys in life, you will find yourself very connected. The more vulnerable you are in your conversations, the more attached you will become.

The same thing happens physically. The more vulnerable you become, seeing and touching more of each other's bodies in loving ways, the more you will become bonded to each other. If you carry that farther, then a deep connectedness will develop between the two of you.

You must not connect deeply to every man you date. Make sure you're really right for each other. If you jump into bed with any man (or, worse, a series of men), not only are you risking getting a sexually transmitted disease but also you'll find yourself being pulled apart emotionally as you violate your moral principles and the Bible's clear teaching. Work on your boundaries; mentally set your stop lines before you go on a date.

Living together. You probably wouldn't want your teenagers to live with someone before they were married. But sometimes people do very strange things because they think they're in love. Don't let some guy move in with you, and don't accept any offers for you and your children to move in with him.

Living together is not a positive way to decide whether to marry a person. Living together eliminates the possibility of dating any other man, and it makes it difficult or almost impossible to leave the relationship. You may find yourself marrying the person because you feel obligated—not because he is the right person for you.

Living together does not test whether a marriage will work or not. Living together has no commitment; therefore, it's very different from marriage. In marriage you make the decision to stay together no matter what test you face as a couple. In living together you make the decision to stay together until it becomes too difficult. It's not a test at all of whether a *marriage* would work. A better test of future marital success is your ability to resolve problems and to be honest with each other.

Mistakes women make. In a book titled *Ten Stupid Things Women Do to Mess Up Their Lives,* Laura C. Schlessinger points out that women make many foolish mistakes in their relationships. She lists ten, but we are going to point out just a few that are appropriate as you think about dating:

☐ Stupid courtship: A woman becomes desperate to have a man—a beggar, not a chooser, in the dating ritual.

☐ Stupid devotion: Women are driven to love and succor (or do you spell that "sucker"?) in vain.

☐ Stupid passion: Women have sex too soon, too romantically, and set themselves up to be burned.

☐ Stupid cohabitations: Stop lying to yourself! You're not living with him because you love him. You're living with him because you hope he'll want you!

☐ Stupid expectations: Some women use marriage as a quick fix for low or no self-esteem.

☐ Stupid forgiving: You don't know when to break off a no-win relationship or how not to get involved in the first place.[2]

Most of the mistakes a woman makes in the area of dating and sex are connected to insecurity. If a woman feels good about who she is becoming, if she has a number of friends of both sexes who are supportive of her growth and if she has a vital relationship with God, she is not going to be manipulated by a man into some of these stupid mistakes. The insecure woman who does not have a life of her own looks to events and other people to meet her needs; she'll grab any rope thrown to her by a man, because she doesn't know how to swim on her own.

Another response that an insecure woman may make is to control. The controlling woman does not appear to be insecure, because she manages things so well. And certainly not every woman who is a good manager is a controller. But sometimes to cover up insecurity and to guarantee that life will not be out of control, a woman becomes a compulsive controller.

The controlling woman can be death to a dating relationship because everything must flow around *her*—her schedule, her moods, her tastes and her fatigue level. The controlling woman loses spontaneity. She finds it difficult to go to a different movie from what she had planned, to eat at a different restaurant or even to go on a surprise date. Her automatic control mode may drive men away because they feel to have a relationship with her would mean losing their own identity and personality.

Trust—the antidote. It is totally understandable why a woman would feel insecure if she has unresolved childhood issues, feels a sense of unfulfillment in life in general and has been abandoned by her husband. She is likely to either react to men with fierce independence or attempt to be a savage controller.

For many women, marriage was a way of controlling life. It gave stability, a sense of direction, purpose and mission. But abandonment destroyed the foundations of security. Part of Ann's way of coping when her life seemed out of control was to withdraw. Another way she handled the loss of control was to determine not to date any men or even to trust men. But suddenly, Philip changed the controlled environment she had created. She was excited as well as fearful. Her question was what she should do about Philip. But in reality, she needed to answer the question, *What should I do about my life now that it again seems to be out of control?*

The solution is not to focus on men as the saviors of a confused life, nor to focus on the past pain of marriage or childhood abandonment experiences. The answer is to focus on trusting God and accepting his direction and peace in your life.

Jesus says: "So my counsel is: Don't worry about *things*—food, drink, and clothes. . . . Will all your worries add a single moment to your life?" (Mt 6:25, 27).

He continues: "But your heavenly Father already knows perfectly well that you need them, and he will give them to you if you give him first place in your life and live as he wants you to. So don't be anxious about tomorrow. God will take care of your tomorrow too. Live one day at a time" (Mt 6:32-34).

Jesus is trying to focus us away from our attempt to control circumstances. He wants us to trust him. He wants us to believe that God not only understands our needs but is going to meet those needs.

We have a gray cat named Mon Ami (French for "my friend"). She doesn't seem to worry much about whether we remember to buy cat food for her or take her to the vet or wash her little blanket that fits in the tray on Sally's desk.

No, Mon Ami simply climbs up on Sally's desk, goes over to her tray and curls up in total security. Just before she drops off to sleep, she murrs a few times just to let you know that she's glad you're there.

We humans could use a little bit more of Mon Ami's trust. God already knows our needs, and he wants to meet them. Perhaps all we need to do is to say thank you a few times.

For the Lord says, "Because she loves me, I will rescue her; I will make her great because she trusts in my name. When she calls on me I will answer; I will be with her in trouble, and rescue her and honor her. I will satisfy her with a full life and give her my salvation." (Ps 91:14-16, adapted)

— Part Five —

PREVENTING ABANDONMENT

I t may seem strange at this point in the book, after talking about an abandonment that has already occurred, to introduce a chapter on preventing it. Our purpose is twofold.

In some women's marriages, there is enough distress to bring on the fear that things *may* fall apart. For these women, there is still time to take steps against abandonment. They need help in how to understand the situation and help their husbands understand it—then there may be hope.

Other women have been through abandonment, have now remarried or come to the point of openness to remarriage—and are terrified that the same thing may happen all over again. They need insights that will help them work against that.

That's why we include here a chapter on making sure history doesn't repeat itself.

—15—

Stop History
from Repeating
Itself

SEVERAL YEARS AGO I (JIM) WAS REFINISHING SOME FURNITURE. THE warning on the can was very clear: "Be sure no wax or oil is on the surface before this finish is applied." Some spots of candle wax had dripped on the wood, but I sanded them several times, hoping that I had removed the wax.

It's very difficult to remove wax from wood, and, sure enough, I didn't get it all. When I put on the stain, it didn't soak into the areas with wax residue. The result was that the top of this oak dresser had a beautiful, dark walnut stain—except for the white spots where the wax had soaked in.

If I had continued with the finishing process, applying several coats of polyurethane, I would have ended up with those ugly white blotches permanently showing. The only solution was to use a finish remover that would also remove the wax. Then I had to resand the whole top. If I had done the surface correctly the first time, I wouldn't have had to go through all of these extra steps.

The focus of this chapter is on two different women—the married woman who fears abandonment and the divorced woman who is open to the possibility of remarriage. If a woman will focus on preventing abandonment, she may be able to eliminate future grief and pain.

With prevention as the goal, let's look at three major areas concerning your current husband or a man you might choose as a future husband:

☐ His potential for abandoning you
☐ Your growth in understanding men and life
☐ The environment surrounding your marriage

If you're careful about these areas, eliminating the negative aspects and encouraging positive growth, you can reduce the possibility of abandonment. We are fully aware that some men will not change or cooperate at all, no matter what you do. But for your own long-term health, you must be able to say you really did your best with your current marriage or are well prepared for any future marriage.

His Potential for Abandoning You

In a sense, each man has an "abandonment-potential quotient." A trained counselor can often spot the likelihood that a man will abandon his wife. It's important for a wife to understand her husband's potential so that she can help her husband mature and reduce his likelihood of abandonment. Obviously, the man too needs to understand his own potential for walking out so he can work against it.

In fact, this understanding should take place before the couple is married. If the likelihood of abandonment is quite high, the smart woman will not go through with marriage. Some women, however, marry extremely needy men. Sometimes, these women are doing social work rather than marrying an equal partner! To understand your man's abandonment potential, it's important to look at the following areas.

His background. Study his parents' and grandparents' marriages. Is there an environment of respect, security and commitment by the men in the family toward their wives? Or are they flirtatious, constantly on the prowl for other women? Have they been involved in affairs?

Your man's home environment is going to have an automatic influence on his life. You will see that influence being expressed in the way he treats his mother, other women and you. Unless there is some strong intervening force in your husband's life, he is likely to duplicate the environment in which he was raised.

His friends. A second strong influence will be the male friends he draws around himself. Are they men who treat women with dignity? Are the married men in the group faithful to their wives? Is there a flow of dirty stories and putdowns of women?

When a man has a pattern of diminishing women, he will easily step across the line to devaluing his wife as soon as the fascination of sex has lessened. A man's friends either reinforce his devaluing background or help him break free from it.

His connection to God. Your husband may have come from a family of men who abandoned their wives or were likely to abandon them. If so, there's a high possibility that he will duplicate that pattern. However, if he is strongly connected to God, then God will continually influence his belief structure. What he believes about life and people will ultimately work itself out in the way he acts. In short, the more a man believes the biblical teachings on marriage commitment, the less likely he is to abandon you.

So, what kind of guy is he? Even if his home was a bad one, has he chosen different friends and has he chosen to make a stand for what God wants in his life?

Crucial questions. Earlier in this book we considered the general question "Why do men abandon women?" We looked at the times of life when a man is likely to abandon a woman and why he would choose to. In addition, we explored some of the reasons why a woman can become undesirable to her husband.

By understanding why and when men abandon women, a woman can be prepared ahead of time for likely times for abandonment, and she can modify any negative patterns in herself to reduce the likelihood of becoming undesirable.

But what about *his* negative patterns? A word of caution: don't get trapped in the *what he should be* mindset. Continually work with *what is.* And certainly don't marry a man thinking you can reform him. Each person in a marriage adapts to be more compatible with the other, but these changes are usually quite small. Don't count on massive changes.

When we speak to men, at men's retreats or in private counseling, we confront them with the issues men have trouble with in marriage, such as talking about feelings, listening to their wives, commitment, personal growth and adapting to meet their wives' needs. But the focus in this book is on you, the woman reader. You must keep focused on *what is* and not what you wish it could be.

What do men need to change? First, women need to identify areas where men should be encouraged to change so they are less prone to abandon a wife. Then they can affirm the men in these areas.

1. Value women as equals. If a man views a woman as inferior, he is more likely to use her and throw her away when his need for her is finished. God has not made men and women the same, but he has given each of us abilities and insights that we need to use to nourish each other.

2. Learn from women. As a man becomes teachable and a woman contributes insights or skills that help him accomplish

his goals, she becomes more important to him and less likely to be abandoned. I have become a better speaker, writer, father, grandfather and man because of what Sally has contributed to my life. She has encouraged and coached—and pushed me at times—and I am the better for it.

3. Good friends. The qualities of friendship, such as availability, confidentiality, trust, affirmation, acceptance and an enriching love for the other person, tend to bond a couple closely together so that abandonment is less likely.

4. Expressing feelings. The man who is able to express his feelings to a woman crosses over an important line of intimacy and bonding. If she expresses affirmation and sensitivity toward his feelings, the two can develop a deep closeness that is less likely to be broken by abandonment.

What can a woman do to help her man? It's best to view any helping in terms of friends helping each other. A good friend urges, gives information, helps to arrange opportunities for growth—but never demands growth. A good friend always realizes that ultimately the other person has the full choice. Only the other person can decide to grow or not. So what can a woman do?

1. Pray. Make the critical connection for growth in your husband by asking God to create a desire within him for growth and change.

2. Appreciate. People like to have their shoulders massaged. Most people respond with, "That really feels good—thank you!" The physical massage is similar to verbal encouragement—people enjoy it and want more.

People tend to grow in the direction in which they are affirmed. Affirm your man in areas that will increase his stability. For example, if you are at a social gathering and one of the men starts to talk crudely about women, but your husband doesn't join in, tell him afterward how much you appreciated that. Tell him you admire him for not being a crude man but a person who sees the worth of every individual.

Or tell him how glad you are that he is not like his father or your uncle who talks crudely or has left his wife. Look for opportunities to affirm him in the direction of strength, and he will tend to keep going in those positive directions.

Clearly settle in your mind the difference between manipulating your man for your benefit and being the "wind" of encouragement in his sails, enabling him to fully accomplish his goals for his personal growth.

3. Encourage him to relate to men of high quality. But don't nag him about it. Instead, when your man has any connection with other men of moral strength, affirm him. "I'm glad that you and Mike seem to be hitting it off. You seem to have a lot in common. Maybe we ought to get together as couples once in a while."

Sometimes a man needs a little help to make the transition to a new experience. An appropriate word from you to a key man whom your husband respects may prompt that man to invite your husband to a men's weekend retreat, a men's breakfast or a major men's rally such as Promise Keepers. Avoid actions like this if your husband is likely to feel you have been sneaky or manipulative!

Remember, friends don't force their friends to grow or slow down their growth. They provide opportunities: "Honey, I know that you've been stressed about our finances. Our lack of money seems to be the reason why you're not going to the men's weekend retreat. I've been saving money for something special for you. So—if you'd like to go—here's the registration fee for the weekend, as my gift to you."

You can help reduce the likelihood of abandonment by cooperating with God as he works within your husband to help him mature.

Your Growth in Understanding Men and Life

Certainly your husband is a major factor in the potential for abandonment. But you are another main element. Are you growing and changing as your marriage grows and changes? Or are you becoming a contributor to a future abandonment? Let's focus on a few areas.

Growing. We encouraged you earlier to grow so that you'll continue to be an interesting person. Keep pace and encourage your man so that your individual growth is an assistance to a stronger marriage. Some of the goals of your growth should be:

□ Become self-assured. As women progress through life, most move from being the child of their mother and father to being the girlfriend of several boys and then to being the wife of a husband. The question is, have you arrived at an identity that is your own? Are you only the extension of someone else's personality? Does your life have meaning only because of someone else's existence?

To prevent abandonment, you must learn to clearly understand the special gifts that God has given you to enrich other people. Make use of those gifts! Take initiative. Be creative. Don't always stay in the shadow of your husband—or anyone else. By the time a maturing man reaches his forties, a self-assured woman of poise is going to be more desirable than an insecure woman who has not had a new thought in years.

□ Know your boundaries. A woman with undefined emotional boundaries allows people to run over her. She tends to be used by people and treated with less respect by her husband. That lack of respect makes it easier for him to abandon her. As a woman becomes more aware of who she is as God's special creation, it is easier for her to focus her life on her priorities and say no to unnecessary tasks, to other people's deadlines or emergencies. A woman who knows her boundaries is not selfish but serves people in line with God's purposes for her.

☐ Deal with your childhood emotional baggage. Were you a victim of sexual molestation, physical violence or verbal abuse? Did you come from a broken home or was a parent an alcoholic? Whatever baggage you are carrying from childhood, get the professional help you need to resolve it.

We have worked with lots of couples whose marriages are breaking up because the husband is emotionally exhausted from trying to live with a wife who has unresolved childhood baggage. Husbands tell us: "There is a rage about her. She has to control everything we do. It's difficult for her to be spontaneous. She's very insecure about raising our children. I think she wants to be married to me, but she keeps me at arm's length. I always feel insecure about her love for me. She continually thinks I will be like her father, who was unfaithful to her mother. She is preoccupied with her past and doesn't seem to be getting any better."

To prevent abandonment (and for your own health and happiness as well), work on your problems with help from a counselor, a twelve-step program or a healing prayer group so that you and your man won't be emotionally worn out by your past. He may love you very deeply and may not want to abandon you, but he may not be able to handle all the stress from your past.

Adapt to life. In chapter four we talked about the various seasons of life when a woman might be abandoned. Marriages succeed only as people continue to adjust and meet each other's needs.

We are very different today from the Jim and Sally who married years ago. In fact, we probably are married to the fifth different Jim and Sally! As each season of life has turned us into different people, our marriage has had to change as well. Review the chapter entitled "When a Woman Becomes Disposable." Talk with a couple of women friends about the life stage you're in now and the one that is coming, so that you'll know how to adapt and reduce the likelihood of abandonment.

Be spiritually alive. It's not enough just to be doing the things mentioned above. We have known several abandoned women who have been growing, adapting, multifocused and physically active but who have a sullenness about them. They are dreadful people to be with. Some of their pet phrases are "Everything in life is rotten," and "Life is hell and then you die."

The best way to adapt to life's changes and demands is to be vitally in touch with God. It will help you have a more positive outlook on life. An attitude of hope makes you more fun to be around. Other people feel lifted by your personality, because your hope is contagious. As you are a person of positive spiritual strength, you will reduce the likelihood of being abandoned.

What do men want? Over the years we've worked with literally thousands of couples whose marriages are stressed. The common complaints about wives that we hear from men at conferences, in counseling sessions and through surveys are:

☐ She does not understand or meet my needs.

☐ She is not a growing and adapting person.

☐ Her physical body is out of control (generally weight gain).

☐ Her world is too small.

We've made a number of comments throughout the book about the first three of these items, but let's think here about life focus. A person with a small world is one who is a mother and wife only—or a career woman only. A person makes a better marriage partner when he or she has several interests in life. For example, a woman whose major emotional energy and time are focused on her career, or whose energy goes totally into raising her children, subtly communicates to her husband that she has no time for companionship with him.

A man in his twenties and thirties may not be bothered by a lack of companionship because of his own career focus. But the single-focused woman is going to be in trouble by the time her husband reaches forty. He is going to want her to be a lover, companion and friend, not just a mother or business executive. So don't feel guilty if you have many interests. You will likely reduce the abandonment potential if you are multifaceted and continue to offer interesting companionship to your husband.

The Environment Surrounding Your Marriage

No, we're not talking about the trees or pollution, smog or contaminated water. We're talking about the environment in which your marriage exists. You and your family live in a certain town or city. You have your jobs with certain coworkers. You're a part of certain social groupings in your community, your church and the schools your kids attend. All of these people and institutions, as well as the physical surroundings, are part of your environment.

Now ask yourself, "What if someone picked up my marriage and family and dropped us in Nairobi, Kenya? How would my life change?" Or what if you were dropped into the quaint city of Montreaux on Lake Geneva in Switzerland? Or what would your family be like if you lived in the huge metropolis of Rio de Janeiro, Brazil, with its nude beaches and fast life?

Take a few minutes to think about your environment. How can it be changed or modified so that your likelihood of being abandoned will be reduced? Let's look at a few areas to prompt your thinking:

Social groups. Who do you spend time with socially—that close inner circle of friends? Next, identify people you know casually; finally, think about the community's influence on you and your family.

Now begin to analyze specific people and the way they influence you. Is their overall affect on you and your family encouraging your marriage stability, or are they subtly promoting abandonment?

Let's get specific. When you're out with close friends, is there a lot of flirting, inappropriate touching and joking going on between people who are not married to each other? What about church? Is there an inordinate amount of "greeting each other with a holy kiss" or inappropriate hugging that has nothing to do with spiritual warmth but everything to do with sexual appetite?

Take a hard look at the social groupings around you. If you feel uneasy about any person or group of people, listen to your inner voice. It is the quiet prompting of God, warning you away from potential danger.

Work. A major factor in your environment is your work. Make the same type of assessment of each person in the work environment as in your social groupings. Are your and your husband's coworkers the kind who encourage stability in marriage, or are they subtly influencing you or your husband to be open to moving on to someone new?

You may not be able to change your job, but you may be able to avoid the people in that job who are most offensive. It may be possible to develop a group that focuses on marriage stability in spite of other coworkers who are inclined toward infidelity. If your husband is aware of these dangers, he can take the same precautions.

Aging. Then there is the internal environment within each of you. As you age, you look at life differently. We have examined some of the different ways men look at life as they age. This changing internal environment will require you to focus on your husband's changing needs as well as your own.

Evil. The Bible warns very clearly, "Be careful—watch out for attacks from Satan, your great enemy. He prowls around like a hungry, roaring lion, looking for some victim to tear apart" (1 Pet 5:8).

It would be naive to believe that our environment consists

only of the people, events and things that we see around us. A spiritual dimension—both good and evil—influences your environment. Clearly, Satan is trying to destroy your marriage, reduce your effectiveness as a person, break your hope for living and discourage you from serving God.

On the other hand, God is working. Think about the special people he has brought into your circle of friendship. Reflect on the insights that you're getting from the Bible, from your small study group, from church or from your circle of close friends. All of these are the activity of God, trying to strengthen your marriage or prepare you for a future marriage.

A war is going on between good and evil in your environment, and you're caught in the middle. But remember the Bible says clearly, "You . . . are from God and have overcome them, because the one who is in you is greater than the one who is in the world" (1 Jn 4:4 NIV).

How do you reduce the likelihood of abandonment taking place? Maybe this story will help. I (Sally) was leading a women's retreat in Colorado. During the retreat I became close friends with many of the women. One woman talked to me about her previous involvement in Satan worship. She eventually became a leader in the cult. Then she became a Christian and her life changed dramatically.

After we talked about something that was of concern to her, I asked, "Could I ask a question? I've heard stories that people who are Satan worshipers pray that Christian marriages will be destroyed.

"One of the stories I've heard was about a Christian man who was served dinner on an airline flight. The man next to him refused the meal, saying, 'I'm fasting.' The Christian man thought perhaps he was seated next to another Christian, so he said, 'I notice you're fasting; are you a Christian?' The man replied, 'No, I'm a Satanist, and today we are praying that marriages of

Christian leaders will be destroyed.' "

I continued telling my Colorado friend, "Well, after I heard that story, I told Jim what I had heard. He thought that someone was making this up or exaggerating. So, my question for you: Is the story true? Do Satan worshipers really pray against the marriages of Christian leaders?"

My new friend responded forcefully, "Oh, Sally, what you heard is absolutely true! When I was a Satanist, we had regular rituals to pray that marriages would be destroyed. In fact, that's one of the reasons I faithfully pray for James Dobson, Chuck Swindoll and the two of you, because I know that wicked people are praying against you.

"Satan worshipers know that if they can destroy the marriage of a leader couple, they can also destroy that couple's work and cause their followers to be disillusioned. So I want you to know that I pray for you every day."

How do we minimize the potential for abandonment? The answer is found in allowing God to empower you to fully understand the abandonment potential of your husband, to understand how you should be growing and changing, and then, fully aware of your environment, to pray for God's good purposes to unfold in your life.

You are not alone! God has given you his Holy Spirit, the Scriptures and Christian friends to help you as you work either to prevent abandonment or to be able in good conscience to *move on after he moves out.*

Lord, with all my heart I thank you. I will sing your praises. . . . When I pray, you answer me, and encourage me by giving me the strength I need. (Ps 138:1, 3)

—Epilogue—

Whatever Happened to Ann?

*C*HRISTOPHER HAYES IS THE DIRECTOR OF PROJECT PACE, A PEER counseling program for older adults in Orange County, California. Hayes was interviewed by the San Diego *Union-Tribune* about the work he has done with abandoned women.

Hayes said he found the 352 divorced women whom he surveyed not to be lonely or bitter. Many had started new careers, and very few said that they were afraid of aging alone or were wanting to get married again.

One of the women in the study said, "My life did not end four years ago; a new and wonderful and exciting life began. Not only am I a more interesting person, but I am also stronger, freer and very capable of taking care of myself."

Hayes went on to say, "This is not to say that all of the women faced zero problems. Many initially were devastated by divorce, particularly when their husbands abandoned them. A large percentage of the women also faced a dramatic drop in income, and few were savvy about financial affairs."

Hayes and coauthors Deborah Anderson and Melinda Blau have summarized their findings in *Our Turn: The Good News About Women and Divorce*. He emphasized that they were not recommending divorce as the path to happiness—their purpose in the book was to debunk some of the common myths about mid-life divorced women. "They are not only surviving, they're thriving."

We selected the following myths from the article:

☐ *"It's too late for women to change if they're divorced and over forty*. Not only do they change their lives, they actually grow more adaptable as they age." The authors pointed out that 87 percent of the women surveyed said they have a more positive self-image after divorce.

☐ *"Divorce debilitates women and causes them to lose control over their lives*. On the contrary, two-thirds of the respondents said the process inspired them to gain control over their lives for the first time."

☐ *"The dream of every divorced woman is remarriage*. In fact, 75 percent of the respondents said they desired private, independent time to get to know themselves better. Of women between the ages of fifty and fifty-nine, almost half said they would prefer to remain single for good."

☐ *"Divorced women are lonely."* In fact, they have "a wider circle of friends than ever."

☐ *"Mid-life and older women 'live through' their children after divorce."* "The subject of children rarely even came up in the survey."

☐ *"Divorced women fear age."* Respondents were asked, " 'When you look ahead to retirement years, what do you see?' Nearly half of the respondents checked 'Good health and productivity,' and 70 percent envisioned 'Involvement in interesting activities.' "

Hayes summed up the results of the study by giving the major reason why he felt these abandoned women were doing so well: they found support. "While mid-life divorced women may need help from men [in the financial area of their lives], men could also learn something important from the women. In nearly every case he studied, women were able to make the divorce transition successfully, thanks to the support of women friends.

"Women have this incredible way of building a support system that men don't have," Hayes said. "These support systems boost your self-esteem and serve as a bastion in the sea of change. A lot of the women we studied were courageous. Men have a long way to go."[1]

So What Did Happen to Ann?

Ann fits the characteristics pointed out in the study by Hayes. Initially, as you have seen in the book, she was devastated—and for a time really disabled. But gradually she was able to work her way through the abandonment.

Bob did follow through with the divorce, and he did marry Jennifer. The settlement required him to pay child support and, fortunately, he did that. The money from Bob supplemented Ann's accounting salary so that, by downsizing their lifestyle and moving to a smaller house, she was able to make it.

She kept her accounting job but gradually realized that she was becoming more people-oriented than number-oriented. So, once the children were older, she decided to enter school part-time to work on a master's degree in counseling.

Ann had the advantage of a large support network with strong connections to family and friends who helped her recover and encouraged her continued growth. She found a strong divorce-recovery group. She continued to spend priority time with her children. She became involved with several other abandoned women. Later, as part of her training, she started three small groups for women struggling with marital problems, abandonment and recovery.

Four years later Ann graduated with her master's degree. She was a mid-life woman with life experience who was leading recovery groups. As a result, she was offered a full-time job as an intern. A year and a half later, after she was licensed, she was invited into the counseling center as a partner.

At age forty-five, Ann is a very different woman from the Ann who was devastated by her husband's abandonment. She possesses serenity, poise and a depth of understanding that draws others to her. Her insights about people help her in counseling. Ann isn't just a passive counselor, listening to people's problems; she understands women and knows what they need to accomplish to become whole persons.

Kim is in college and Shawn in high school. Both of them have been marked by their father's abandonment, but it has made them more sensitive to people's needs. They understand why it happened and what their mother went through to recover from abandonment. Neither of them fears marriage. If they choose to marry, it will be with an insight that few young people have.

Ann didn't marry Philip. She is still involved with many men as friends, but she doesn't feel a desperate, driving need to be married. She is very secure and happy with where she is in life, where her children are and the impact that she's able to have in other people's lives.

Ann truly has become what the Scripture describes:

She is a woman of strength and dignity, and has no fear of old age. When she speaks, her words are wise, and kindness is the rule for everything she says. . . . Charm can be deceptive and beauty doesn't last, but a woman who fears and reverences God shall be greatly praised. (Prov 31:25-26, 30)

Notes

Chapter Three: The Roses Are Dead—But the Thorns Still Cut
[1]Faith H. Leibman, "Childhood Abandonment/Adult Rage: The Root of Violent Criminal Acts,"*American Journal of Forensic Psychology* 4 (1992): 57-64.

Chapter Four: When a Woman Becomes Disposable
[1]Ellyn Bader and Peter T. Pearson, *In Quest of the Mythical Mate: A Developmental Approach* (New York: Brunner/Mazel, 1988).

[2]For helpful information regarding menopause, read Sally's book *Menopause: Help and Hope for This Passage* (Grand Rapids, Mich.: Zondervan, 1990).

[3]Three helpful books about the stages of life are the following: William Lee Carter, *Family Cycles: How Understanding the Way You Were Raised Will Make You a Better Parent* (Colorado Springs: NavPress, 1993); Frank and Mary Alice Minirth, Brian and Deborah Newman, Robert and Susan Hemfelt, *Passages of Marriage: Five Growth Stages That Will Take Your Marriage to Greater Intimacy and Fulfillment* (Nashville: Thomas Nelson, 1991); H. Norman Wright, *Seasons of a Marriage* (Ventura, Calif.: Regal, 1982).

Chapter Five: The Many Faces of Abandonment
[1]Jim Conway, *Adult Children of Legal or Emotional Divorce* (Downers Grove, Ill.: InterVarsity Press, 1990), pp. 33-34.

Chapter Seven: Shock
[1]"Cardiologist Studies Effect of Prayer on Patients," *Brain/Mind Bulletin* 2, no. 7 (1986): 1. See also Randolph C. Byrd, "Positive Therapeutic Effects of Intercessory Prayer in a Coronary Care Unit Population," *Southern Medical Journal* 81, no. 7 (1988): 826-29.

Chapter Eight: Restore the Relationship If Possible

[1]Helpful books in this area include the following:

David Augsburger, *Caring Enough to Forgive/Not Forgive* (Ventura, Calif.: Regal, 1981).

Dave Carder, *Torn Asunder* (Chicago: Moody, 1992).

Gary Chapman, *Hope for the Separated* (Chicago: Moody Press, 1982).

Jim Conway, *Men in Mid-Life Crisis* (Elgin, Ill.: Cook, 1978).

Jim and Sally Conway, *Traits of a Lasting Marriage* (Downers Grove, Ill: InterVarsity Press, 1991).

Sally Conway, *Your Husband's Mid-Life Crisis* (Elgin, Ill.: Cook, 1980, rev. 1987).

Sally Conway and Jim Conway, *When a Mate Wants Out* (Grand Rapids, Mich.: Zondervan, 1992).

Ron Durham, *Happily Ever After and Other Myths About Divorce* (Wheaton, Ill.: Victor, 1993).

S. D. Gaede, *For All Who Have Been Forsaken* (Grand Rapids, Mich.: Zondervan, 1989).

George S. Pransky, *Divorce Is Not the Answer* (Blue Ridge Summit, Penn.: TAB Books, 1990).

Larry Richards, *When It Hurts Too Much to Wait* (Dallas: Word, 1985).

Lewis B. Smedes, *Forgive and Forget: Healing the Hurts We Don't Deserve* (New York: Pocket Books, 1984).

Jim Talley, *Reconcilable Differences* (Nashville: Thomas Nelson, 1991).

Ed Wheat, *How to Save Your Marriage Alone* (Grand Rapids, Mich.: Zondervan, 1983).

Chapter Nine: From Pain to Acceptance

[1]Elisabeth Kübler-Ross, *On Death and Dying* (New York: Macmillan, 1969).
[2]Conway, *Adult Children of Legal or Emotional Divorce*, p. 212. See the whole chapter on forgiving the past, pp. 205-20.

Chapter Twelve: Children

[1]These ideas are taken from Ross Campbell, *How to Really Love Your Child* (Wheaton, Ill.: Victor, 1977), and have been proven by the Conways through years of experience.

Chapter Fourteen: Dating and Sex

[1]Jim Conway and Sally Conway, *Sexual Harassment No More* (Downers Grove,

Ill.: InterVarsity Press, 1993), p. 168.

[2]Paraphrased from Nicole Brodeur, "Dr. Laura Schlessinger," *The Orange County Register,* April 12, 1994, p. 2.

Epilogue: Whatever Happened to Ann?

[1]Barbara Fitzsimmons, "Older Divorcees Find New and Better World All by Themselves," *The Orange County Register,* June 5, 1993, p. E-1.

Jim Conway, Ph.D., and Sally Christon Conway, M.S.

Jim and Sally are cofounders of Mid-Life Dimensions/Christian Living Resources, Inc., a California-based organization that offers help to people struggling to save or rebuild their marriages.

Jim and Sally speak together at colleges, seminaries, churches and retreat centers. They also appear on many radio and television programs. They previously were speakers on their own national daily radio program, *Mid-Life Dimensions,* broadcast on more than two hundred stations.

Jim served as a pastor for almost thirty years, while Sally served as pastor's wife. Sally also has been an elementary-school remedial reading specialist. For five years Jim directed the Doctor of Ministry program at Talbot School of Theology, Biola University, and was associate professor of practical theology. Sally was an adjunct professor at Talbot for five years.

Sally holds a bachelor of science degree in elementary education and a master of science degree in human development. Jim holds two earned doctorates—a D.Min. in ministry and a Ph.D. in adult development and learning.

Jim and Sally have three daughters, three sons-in-law and several grandchildren.

To contact them about speaking, write them c/o InterVarsity Press, P.O. Box 1400, Downers Grove, IL 60515.